ARNHEIM'S ANSWER

ARNHEIM'S ANSWER

The Secret of Student Success
How Qualifications Are Won

by
MICHAEL T. W. ARNHEIM
Ph.D. (Cantab), LL.B. (Lond), M.A., M.B.A.,
D.B.A., A.C.I.S., A.M.B.I.M.
Sometime Fellow of St. John's College, Cambridge

PAPERFRONTS

ELLIOT RIGHT WAY BOOKS
KINGSWOOD, SURREY, U.K.

Made and Printed in Great Britain by Hunt Barnard Printing Ltd, Aylesbury, Bucks.

CONTENTS

For my nephew
SELWYN BLIEDEN

Knowledge is proud that he has learned so much;
Wisdom is humble that he knows no more.

– William Cowper

HOW TO USE THIS BOOK

Are you a university student, at a college, or a professional student of any kind? If you belong to any of these categories, or even if you are a sixth former, this book is for you.

Written in a lively and straightforward style, it is a practical book which should be your constant companion throughout your student days. It has been written with your needs in mind. Some of the questions it deals with are:

- How your examination is marked – the inside story.
- How to deal with your lecturers and tutors.
- How decisions affecting you are taken – another inside story.
- How to prevent yourself from becoming your own worst enemy.
- How to get the most out of your reading.
- How to take effective notes.
- How to think effectively.
- How to improve your memory.
- How to write effective essays.
- How to prepare for examinations.

After browsing at random, you should read the book through from cover to cover, marking it as you go along. Then reread it bit by bit in whatever order you like according to your problems of the moment and consult it whenever you feel the need for some friendly practical advice.

Part I, "Know Your Enemy", is essentially designed to advise you on how to deal with your examiners and the university or college bureaucracy, your lecturers and tutors, and, not least, how to help yourself most effectively to achieve your goals. The nitty-gritty of how to tackle the varied chores that beset a student's life is dealt with in Part II, "Know-How". The last seven chapters of the book each end with a list of *guidelines* encapsulating the advice of the chapter in a nutshell. These are meant for quick reference after you have read the chapter in question. But they are not intended as a substitute for reading the chapter. Some will prove quite baffling unless the chapter is read first.

The book has been written on the basis of my own experience as a student (with degrees in the humanities, business and law) and over twenty years of teaching at a number of universities, including Cambridge.

Here's hoping you'll use it to the full. Read, profit – and enjoy!

PART ONE

KNOW YOUR ENEMY

CHAPTER I

JUDGING THE JUDGES

Study your examiners as closely as you study your subject

When I turned eight I was given a tortoise as a birthday present – a large, lethargic grey-brown blob doing its best to masquerade as a pet rock. My father promptly named it Ilse, after a girl with a similar temperament whom he had known in his boyhood in Germany.

Before long I was confronted with the inevitable prep-school project: to write an essay on "My Pet". I set to work and religiously chronicled the daily activities (or rather, non-activities) of my sluggish tortoise. My essay was returned to me embellished with a cryptic bright red "sp" repeated several times in the margin. Spelling mistakes? But how could that be? My spelling had always been perfect! Upon closer examination it turned out that there was only one supposed spelling mistake, my tortoise's name, Ilse, which recurred a number of times in the course of the essay. The teacher, unfamiliar with this German name, had assumed that it was wrong and had "corrected" it to an English non-name, Isle!

This incident taught me a lasting lesson: that teachers are not omniscient. But it also brought home to me another more disturbing truth: that there are some teachers to whom it has never occurred that they might be mistaken on any point, no matter how trivial. It is from such teachers – including a far from insignificant proportion of college and university lecturers and professors – that the student is most at risk. But, if such mediocrities pose a threat to students in general, it is the ambitious student, the high flier, who is likely to be most vulnerable.

As an undergraduate I was confronted with something of a dilemma. One of the papers in my History finals was on nineteenth-century European History, including such central topics as the unification of Italy and Germany. But if I was forced to answer a question on either of these subjects in the examination I knew that I would not succeed in getting the First Class that I had set my heart on. The lecturer regarded himself as a specialist in the field, though his publication list was non-existent. His views on the Italian and German questions were taken over bodily from the most recent book on the subject in each case. He was up to date but totally unoriginal. And, as so often happens with unoriginal minds, having embraced someone else's idea his faith in it was unshakeable. It would therefore have been suicidal for a student to argue in an examination answer *against* the lecturer's favoured view. But arguing in favour of it was not much better, as one's answer would then lack originality and could not therefore be awarded a first-class mark!

Was there a way out of this dilemma? As it happens, there were some other areas of the syllabus in which my arch-mediocrity of a lecturer was less interested, less well versed – and less opinionated. Among these were two important areas which (luckily for me) I found absolutely riveting: nineteenth-century Russia and the Austro-Hungarian Empire. I concentrated my efforts upon these topics, praying the while that questions on them would appear in the examination paper. I am glad to say they did!

The moral of the story is therefore: Discover your lecturer's prejudices and, unless you are satisfied with a bare pass, try to sidestep them.

It is of course futile to concentrate on some area of the syllabus which is so obscure as to have practically no chance of being set. This is where the judicious art of "spotting" comes in – the ability to work out from past examination papers and the course itself what is likely to come up in your year.

Grading your examiner

As every schoolboy knows (to coin a phrase), examiners vary in their approach, ranging from the strictness of old Jack Boot, for whom a single comma out of place is enough to earn you eternal damnation, to the leniency of old Tom Fool, who is prepared to give you the benefit of the doubt even if your answer bears an uncanny resemblance to the relevant passage of the prescribed textbook.

An easy way out for the examiner is what I call "blueprint marking". Here the examiner, having set the questions, proceeds to write answers to them himself (with or without the aid of his favourite textbook). This may seem commendable, but the trouble is that once there is a piece of paper embodying *the answer* it is very hard in practice for an examiner to do anything but worship it. What this means is that an answer which reproduces the blueprint will score 100% – and any other answer, whether better or worse than the blueprint, will score close to zero.

The reason for this is really quite simple. The type of examiner who prepares a blueprint in the first place is one who believes there is *a right answer* to every question. But, as we shall see in a later chapter, there is no such thing as a right or wrong answer to any question worth asking – in other words, to any true university-level question. So the blueprint marker is essentially a pedantic mediocrity.   And, precisely because he is such a mediocrity the chances are that a good number of student answers *will* easily surpass the quality of his blueprint. But an answer which is better than the blueprint is likely to suffer as much as – if not more than – one which is really weak.

"In the eyes of mediocrity," it has been truly said, "mediocrity is excellence." So, the chances are that the mediocre examiner will not recognise the superiority of even the most brilliant student answer. But, if he *is* capable of recognising an outstanding student answer, that could be even worse. For then his ego is under attack: a classic case of the "Salieri syndrome".

The Salieri syndrome
Antonio Salieri, whose music is now relegated to the dust-heap of oblivion, was a much-acclaimed and much-decorated composer of the eighteenth century. But, despite the honours showered upon him by his contemporaries, and not least by the Emperor Joseph II and his court at Vienna, he seems to have recognised his own mediocrity and the genius of Mozart, whose fame was to arise only after his death. Such self-criticism, rare in any circumstances, is particularly remarkable in a situation where one is surrounded by public adulation, as Salieri was throughout his long career. Yet, Salieri's modesty in seeing himself for what he really was and refusing to be blinded by flattery manifested itself not in praise of Mozart or even in tolerance but in hostility and intrigue against him behind the scenes, effectively blocking any prospect of a court appointment and consigning Mozart to the penury from which he was never to emerge. It used to be believed that Salieri even caused Mozart's death, though – despite the resuscitation of that claim in Peter Shaffer's powerful play *Amadeus* – this was long ago proved to be a baseless accusation. But the court

composer's hostility to the fiery genius was in stark contrast to his otherwise generous and open-handed nature, especially in regard to struggling young musicians. Indeed, after Mozart's death, it was Salieri who was instrumental in securing an appointment for his son.

Though Mozarts may be few and far between in even the most promising class of university students, most of their examiners will likewise be found to be considerably less accomplished than Salieri, whose compositions included more than thirty operas alone, in addition to innumerable shorter works. In fact, the greater the degree of mediocrity in the examiner, the more intense is his hostility likely to be towards originality in the candidate – and *vice versa*. Which is why those who are the most original themselves tend also to be the most tolerant – even when it comes to criticism of their own ideas. One of the very few such people I have met in my life was my Ph.D. supervisor in Cambridge, the late Professor "Hugo" Jones, who was always open-minded and ready to consider views which disagreed with his (as mine often did). Having himself done battle with the conventional wisdom of the academic establishment, he knew what it was to be original, how rare it was and how vital it was to encourage it.

Salieri's personality was as different from Mozart's as could possibly be imagined. Where the court composer was sober, staid, mature, religious, reliable and conventional, the young genius (who was actually only six years his junior) was flippant, flighty, excitable, rude and infantile. But Salieri's prejudice against Mozart was evidently more intellectual than personal. It was Mozart's musical gifts rather than his brash exterior which earned him Salieri's hostility and aroused that most potent of human emotions, jealousy.

At a dinner party in America I recently found myself seated next to an exceptionally beautiful and charming young lady who had just graduated from one of the most exclusive universities on the Eastern seaboard. When she learnt that I was a university professor, she proceeded to launch into an impassioned total onslaught upon her alma mater. The burden of her attack was on the lack of tolerance which she had experienced on the part of her professors, who had tried to place their students in an intellectual strait-jacket. They had signally failed in her case, but she claimed to be one of the very few exceptions. The technique was quite simple: to reserve good grades for those essays, term-papers and examination answers which agreed with *their* views. I was not altogether surprised as I had myself witnessed a similar form of intellectual intolerance in a highly politicised university abroad, where the students soon realised what the party line was that they were expected to toe – and the dire fate that awaited them if they failed to do so. The fact that the party line was ostensibly "liberal" was ironic but did not diminish the reality of the intolerance.

Prejudice
Examinations can even be used as an instrument of policy. There is nothing more cosmopolitan than human anatomy. In Brazil as much as in Belgium, in China as much as in Canada, people tend to be born with ten fingers and ten toes, and one might expect the whole basis of medical science to be the same all over the world. Yet, in practice, even perfectly adequate medical qualifications from one country are often not recognised in another. The real reason is either national, racial or religious prejudice, or else simply market forces: no-one welcomes a sudden inrush of competitors, especially where the size of the market is not growing at the same speed as the competition. This is understandable enough, but for some reason very few authorities are prepared to come out into the open with their true motivation. They prefer instead to use a lot of obfuscating language and rational-looking barriers – including examinations. A medical friend of mine who wanted to emigrate to an English-speaking country which shall be nameless came up against this hurdle. The country in question required medically qualified immigrants to sit a battery of professional examinations, plus an examination in the English language. My friend was English-speaking and so was exempted from the language examination, and, having been in practice for some years, found the professional examinations easy enough. To his surprise, when the results were announced he found that he had failed in everything – including the English-language paper which he had not sat!

There is, however, a form of prejudice which is probably more prevalent than any kind of blanket or group prejudice and even more damaging, and that is personal prejudice. In a university with which I was once associated the students clamoured continually for the introduction of an examination system under numbers rather than names, as already existed in many other educational institutions and examining bodies around the world. After much humming and hawing, the university authorities eventually came out with an "agreement in principle" to a no-name examination system but "regretted" that "technical reasons" prevented their implementing any such system "in the foreseeable future". When pressed still further, they instituted a "commission of enquiry" made up entirely of members of their own group, who finally produced a report flatly denying that there was any "significant" amount of prejudice in their institution and that it was therefore quite unnecessary to depart from the time-honoured system of requiring every student to identify himself on every examination answer submitted.

If these university authorities really believed their own explanation, they were incredibly naive. All the evidence of research reveals just how subjective the marking basis is in every institution of education or examining body ever scrutinised. Allowing students the protection of anonymity cannot of course combat prejudice in general, only the personal variety – though even that may well survive in the case of small groups where the individual's identity may be revealed by such tell-tale signs as handwriting or even colour of ink. But names may of course be used to serve other purposes besides the identification of individuals. They are often an indication of national origin, religion, sex or even race.

One extreme manifestation of prejudice which I have encountered amongst certain junior members of staff is what one might call the "all-or-nothing" approach to marking. Here the examiner, Ms Jane Jaundice, essentially divides all papers into two classes, "very good" and "very bad". "Very good" answers invariably score 90%, "very bad" ones never more than 10%. Though she always awards more ten percents than nineties, Ms Jaundice cannot be accused of not using the full range of marks available – unlike our old friends Jack Boot and Tom Fool, whose marks tend to cluster around only one of the two poles. And, needless to say, the basis of Jane Jaundice's judgment is invariably purely personal. The beauty of Ms Jaundice's approach is that, even if she has only one question to mark in a whole three-hour examination paper, her 10% is so crippling that it can easily result in reducing a candidate's overall class, or even in failing a student who would otherwise have passed. Take for example a paper where, as is often the case, there are four questions to be answered, all carrying equal marks. The candidate scores 50%, a bare pass, on three of them. If he is awarded Ms Jaundice's standard 10% on her question, the poor wretch's overall mark for the paper as a whole drops from 50%, a pass, to 40%, an irretrievable fail.

A friend of mine who teaches Applied Mathematics at a university which still uses names, freely admits that if he sees the candidates' names he will be bound to be prejudiced in favour of some and against others. To guard against this he makes a point of folding back the answer-book cover before he has a chance to catch a glimpse of the name. He has tested himself and found that his knowledge of the student's identity did indeed make a significant difference to the result. Such honesty is extremely rare amongst university teachers, though my friend's bias is undoubtedly by no means uncommon. In fact, personal prejudice may work in a variety of ways and be motivated by a number of different feelings. Hostility is one, and so is favouritism, but even such emotions as surprise and disappointment may play their part. If the examiner knows Joe Bloggs is a pretty good student and suddenly finds that he has turned in a paper which is not up to his usual high standard, he may over-react and give Bloggs a lower mark than he would have done if the same middling paper had been submitted by an otherwise mediocre student.

It is highly unlikely that your examiner will be biased in favour of odd numbers, or against numbers made up of the same digit repeated, but he could still be biased against the whole of a particular batch, even if no individual names are in evidence. It is not uncommon to find a marked discrepancy between the results of internal and external students, with most internal students getting second-class passes, which are hardly ever awarded to external students. Are the internal students really so much better than their external counterparts? A distinguished professor at an affected university explained the discrepancy to me in psychological terms: the examiners (subconsciously or otherwise) are prejudiced against external students simply because those poor wretches have not had the benefit of being taught by *them*!

Some subjects obviously lend themselves much more readily to prejudice than others. One thinks at once of a subject like English literature, where the canons of criticism are so subjective and the teachers themselves quite likely to be

locked in internecine conflict. In fact, however, there is no
subject which is *not* subjective to at least some degree.

My Applied Mathematician friend is a case in point.
Another friend of mine, a professor of Engineering, an
"exact" subject if ever there was one, recently related an
interesting experience. He was acting as an external examiner
and came across an answer to a mathematical problem to
which the internal examiner had awarded zero. Sure enough,
not only the final answer but the intermediate sub-answers
were all wrong. But my friend did not stop there. He went
right back to the beginning of the question and found that
the candidate had made a single small mistake in copying
down the given information. My friend entered the student's
incorrect data on his computer and ran the program on this
basis. The results he obtained were exactly the same as those
staring up at him from the student's examination answer.
There was no mistake other than the initial miscopied data.
How much should he be penalised for this trivial error? As
the candidate clearly understood how to handle this kind of
problem, my friend considered that he should lose only 10%,
and duly recommended that he be given 90% – instead of the
zero which he had been initially awarded.

Another true examination story involving 90% springs to
mind. The scene: the senior examiner's sumptuous set of rooms
in one of the older Cambridge colleges. The subject under
discussion: the so-called General Paper, an examination in
which you were required to spend the whole three-hour period
on a single essay chosen from a number of general topics not
necessarily connected with your subject in any way. As was
customary, each candidate would be considered in turn, with
the discussion going around the table starting with the newest
and most junior examiner present. On the occasion in question
the candidate under consideration was a brilliant student who
was later justifiably to make his mark as a noted academic
and author. The junior examiner, a man of no particular dis-
tinction, started the ball rolling by making a few vaguely flat-
tering but essentially non-committal remarks about the candidate's essay and ended by recommending a mark of 70%. The
tone of the comments and the recommended marks inched
upwards as the discussion went round the table, until the senior
examiner's turn came around. His remarks were brief:
"Ninety," is all he said: "It should be published."

The point is that to the lack-lustre junior examiner the

brilliant undergraduate posed a threat, but the senior examiner, himself an accomplished author and charismatic teacher, could afford to give the young man his due.

What you can do about it

Jumping to conclusions is probably the commonest form of exercise in the modern world. So, before taking your examiner to task – or to court – try putting him to the test. What you have taken to be an expression of his prejudice may in reality be nothing more than a reflection of your own ineptitude.

It is much easier to test the marker of a tutorial essay than the person who grades your final examination paper. But even that is fraught with legal problems. A favourite student ploy is to borrow an essay written on the same subject by a member of last year's class, copy it out in your own hand-writing and just change the name on the front. If you have been getting marks in the forties and last year's essay was awarded, say, seventy percent by the same tutor, you are all set. If the borrowed essay *now* gets only forty-five percent, you will know you are being discriminated against – or at least that your tutor has no consistent standard of marking. The snag is that if you try to present the evidence to some higher authority, you may well find yourself in more trouble for cheating than your tutor for dishonest marking.

An American student was convinced that his tutor was grading him according to some preconceived impression and was not even bothering to read his essays through. He hit upon a playful control by drawing a box in the margin of one of the later pages of his next essay and marking it: "Check here if you have read this far."

Sometimes, however, you will be unpleasantly surprised by a tutor or lecturer who is just a little *more* alert than you had anticipated. This was the experience of certain American students living in a fraternity house where there had been a long-standing tradition that any essay (or "term-paper", as they call it) awarded a B or more would be put into a common pool for the use of future generations of fraternity brothers. One old favourite was an essay on America's rural habitat, which, neatly bound and emblazoned with a picture of a moose on the cover, had regularly obtained its B. But one year it was borrowed by a member of the fraternity who decided to make a few changes to its appearance, including the removal of the picture. It came back with a C and the comment:

"Whatever happened to the moose?"

More seriously, though, if you really are the victim of prejudice, subjective marking, blueprint marking or dishonest
marking of any kind, there is no need to grin and bear it.

*The first thing to do is a little research into the marking
habits of your tutor, lecturer or future examiner.* This may be
done by means of chats with more senior students who have
already gone through the mill, discussions with your contemporaries, and of course reflections upon your own experience.
Here are some of the questions to consider:

*Q.   Does your marker/examiner have a particular axe to grind
and is he intolerant of answers which disagree with him?*

A.   If so, you may decide that the best policy is simply to
conform. This easy way out will probably be most advisable
if you are satisfied with a bare pass. In which case, you must
of course be quite sure in advance exactly *what* your
examiner's predilections are. It certainly won't be in your
interest if you slant your answers in a Marxist direction only
to discover that your examiner is chairman of the local Con-
servative Association. And don't rely on tenth-hand gossip
and rumours for this sort of thing. The only way to be certain
of an intellectual bias is on the basis of actual prejudice which
you yourself or friends of yours have experienced at the hands
of the examiner concerned. Go and have a chat with him if
you *really* want to know what he thinks about anything, but
don't make the (amazingly frequent) infantile mistake of
pumping him on the contents of the examination paper: that
is the surest way to get him to clam up altogether.

It's also vital to be sure *who* the examiner is going to be.
Some institutions obligingly print the names of all examiners
on the question paper, but this is uncommon. Other institutions, notably professional examining bodies, keep the identity of their examiners a dark and closely guarded secret. If
the secret really *is* impenetrable, beware of trying to determine – and to pander to – a particular examiner's bias, unless
the whole institution is *known* to have a specific slant, though
even then the chances are that there will be the odd maverick
examiner who will not toe the party line. Quite often, however, it is easy enough to find out beforehand who your
examiners are going to be – and perfectly legal into the bar-
gain. Yet, in such cases it is surprising how few students ever
go to the trouble of doing the necessary research. When I

was a Cambridge don I always made a point of letting my supervision pupils know the make-up of the firing squad that would be confronting them on the day of doom. Practically none of them knew that the names were listed well in advance in the official university organ known as the *Reporter* which was to be found in every college library.

Q. If your examiner shows no sign of bias as far as the subject is concerned, does he have any other predilections which you should know about?

A. If he is partial – or, perhaps even more important, if he is violently antipathetic – towards a particular colour of ink, that is information you can easily act upon to your advantage. Unfortunately, most prejudices are less easy to accommodate. If, for example, your examiner tends to become more testy as he works his way through a pile of scripts, so that the script which he marks last thing at night – or, more likely, in the wee hours of the morning – is invariably meted out a more savage form of justice than the one he starts his day with, there is nothing you can do about it.

But there are many surprisingly obvious quirks which students fail to take advantage of. One such, which is common in some of the "better" universities as well as in many inferior institutions, is a tendency on the part of certain examiners to be unduly impressed by superficial brilliance of style, sometimes to the point where the content of the answer is almost disregarded. Not a few first class degrees have been earned as a result of this bias! If you have been taught by the examiner concerned, this type of predilection will have become obvious enough. But even if you have never met him, his own writings (if any) should give him away. Do they display a surface sparkle unmatched by any brilliance of thought or insight and lacking in depth? If so, he's your man all right. The solution in this case is to set about deliberately to cultivate an appropriately rich style of writing for examination purposes, even to the point of preparing in advance choice phrases and purple passages which can be adapted for use in a variety of questions.

But beware! For every examiner who drools over rich epithets and lush prose there is probably at least one who becomes nauseous if any such concoction comes within a mile of him. To such an examiner language is not an end in itself but a tool designed to serve a specific purpose – the purpose of communication. Clarity in expressing ideas is seen as the goal, and ornate language which obfuscates instead of illuminating will cost its author dearly. As always, the moral is: do your homework; find out what your examiner's predilections are.

A common prejudice is the petty-language-error fixation, of which there are several varieties. Probably the commonest is the spelling-fixation, where the slightest error in spelling is subconsciously characterised in the examiner's mind as incontrovertible proof of the candidate's illiteracy, and hence of his imbecility. Everything else is ignored, so fixated does the examiner become on these secret touchstones of intellectual bankruptcy.

Another variety is the preposition-fixation, in which any sentence ending with a preposition is likely to cost the candidate a class or two. In colloquial speech, of course, people end sentences with prepositions all the time, and it would be pedantic to insist that it is wrong to say, or even to write, "I could not understand what he was talking *about*." Other preposition-ending usages are much less commendable, such as: "Can you tell me where the football game is *at*?" According to a Harvard story, when a somewhat stuck-up student at that institution was stopped on the street and asked this question by an out-of-town visitor, the student replied by informing his interlocutor that it was wrong to end a sentence with a preposition. The stranger then obligingly rephrased his question: "Can you tell me where the football game is at, asshole?"

Slang is another sore point with the petty-minded, to whom anything smacking of colloquial speech is taboo. It would do little good to point out to such people that language is in a constant state of flux and that today's slang is quite likely to be the staid form of expression of the conservatives of tomorrow (though most slang is in fact pretty transient and appears quaint to the next generation, if it is remembered at all).

It is not always easy to detect in advance whether your examiner suffers from some variety of the petty-language-fixation, unless, again, you have come across him at close quarters, in which case his nit-picking approach to life would have become obvious. But it is easy enough to avoid falling foul of such quirks. If you take care to write good standard English at all times and pay attention to your spelling, you will not only avoid offending the petty-language brigade but you will also create a good impression generally. Some people seem to be naturally good spellers and others naturally atrocious spellers, but even if you are one of the latter the situation is by no means entirely irretrievable.

A painless way of improving your spelling is to keep a dictionary at your elbow whenever you do any writing and to look up in it any word of whose spelling you are *in the least* unsure. A student of mine in Cambridge who was a naturally atrocious speller and who could not be bothered to use a dictionary would leave the writing of his weekly essay to the last minute, when he would hurriedly tap out a few hasty thoughts on his trusty old manual typewriter. Needless to say, the essay was invariably crawling with spelling mistakes ranging from the sublime to the ridiculous. My pupil rather ungallantly blamed the typewriter – something which it is hard to do in an examination which has to be written by hand.

The use of a dictionary to check your spelling may even reveal that you have habitually misspelt some of your favourite words since your earliest childhood. But don't you have to know how a word is spelt *in order* to look it up in the dictionary in the first place? The day is probably not too far off when a computerised dictionary will respond to sound as well as to writing. Those whose spelling sense is so undeveloped that they cannot even begin to use a dictionary will just have to wait until that day comes. In the meantime we can but marvel that they are at least able to read the road-signs leading to the university – for there certainly are some university students who are well-nigh illiterate.

Anyone with even a nodding acquaintance with Latin should have no trouble with English spelling, as most misspelt English words are of Latin origin. Yet it is alarming to find how compartmentalised people's minds can be. I have even come across someone who consistently wrote "independant" (for "independent") and was quite adamant that "accommodate" had only one "m" – and he was a lecturer in a department of Classics!

Q. What about handwriting? Is there anything you can do if your handwriting is bad and the examiner is intolerant of bad handwriting?

A. You can of course request permission to type your examination, and it is as well to be a competent typist before asking – just in case your request is granted. But don't count on it. If yours is a conventional, not to say old-fashioned, institution, the chances of success are slight. You could also go to the other extreme and take up calligraphy, though it is doubtful whether the extra marks earned through this would be enough to outweigh the loss of time in practising it in the examination room. In Cambridge a candidate whose examination script is considered illegible is required to come in again a few days later and dictate it to a typist. It might be thought that this would be a golden opportunity to make any changes in one's script that one liked, but, alas, few scripts are really *so* illegible as to enable a candidate to get away with it.

The medical profession, we know, prides itself on its illegibility, though whether this originated as part of that profession's pathological secretiveness or as an attempt to cover up its ignorance of Latin (the language used in prescriptions) is a moot point. In any event, a medical *student* would be as ill-advised as the student of any other subject to cultivate deliberate illegibility.

It is sometimes suggested that a copper-plate handwriting may actually be a handicap to the examination candidate, as all the weaknesses of his anwers will be readily apparent, while his less than perfectly legible fellow-student will get the benefit of the doubt, so that his equally weak answer will probably earn a higher mark. In my experience this is generally exactly the opposite of the truth. Even the least aesthetically inclined examiner tends to appreciate a neat and legible answer, which is not infrequently subconsciously equated with a neat and orderly mind. There is also a little matter of ego-stroking. An untidy script may well be interpreted – subconsciously, again – as showing a lack of consideration for the examiner, and may easily elicit a decidedly less than charitable response.

But what is the solution for the congenitally untidy? However illegible your handwriting may be, you *will* be able to learn to *print* acceptably – or re-learn, to be precise, as this was probably the way you first learnt to write as a child. I am not now referring to the type of printing sometimes required on official forms, i.e. BLOCK LETTERS, but rather the ordinary type of letters used in printing, with lower-case as well as capital letters. The chief value of this exercise is that the letters are not connected and are therefore likely to be much more legible than your cursive writing. Writing in this way will of course slow you down tremendously, something which may make you reject the whole idea. But I am *not* suggesting that you print the *whole* of an examination answer. Every answer has certain main points, words or phrases which you *really* want your examiner to see. These are the things that should be printed, with the rest written in cursive. If the reason for your untidiness is a large sprawling handwriting, – or even if it isn't – it often helps to write only on every second line. This makes it considerably easier on the eye.

Q. Is it true that humour is best avoided in examination answers?

A.   The short answer to this, as to so many risky practices, is: when in doubt, don't. I have known university teachers who take great delight in finding "howlers" in students' essays and examination scripts. Some of them even keep a special "howler book" in which they enthusiastically enter their new acquisitions as they mark their way through a pile of scripts. But what really makes their day is the howl of delight from their like-minded colleagues when they read out – or, better still, recite – their latest gem in the staff tea-room. The chief difference between this and genuine humour is that howler-collectors laugh at their students, not with them. Howlers tend to be highly unhilarious except to a small knot of devotees. At least some of these howler hobbyists are evidently insecure people who need to bolster their own egos by trampling on those of their students.

Howler-collectors are unlikely to appreciate humour in a student's essay or examination answer. But even if your examiner has a genuine sense of humour it would be unwise to assume that he would appreciate *your* humour. There are some self-styled jokers who are little short of rabid if a member of their audience so much as attempts to tell a joke. This is seen to pose a threat to the omnipotence of the teacher-joker. One such person I encountered was so hostile to anyone else getting in on what he saw as *his* act that every time a member of his adult audience tried to make a humorous remark he would retort that a recent actors' union report disclosed that there were no fewer than 37,000 comedians out of work. He presumably regarded himself as one of the few comedians who had made it, though his adult-education classes were not exactly on Broadway.

CHAPTER II

THE OLDEST PROFESSION

Which has been of greater benefit to mankind, the discovery of fire or the invention of the wheel? It is a moot point. But no discovery or invention is of much use unless it is taught to others. It would not have been enough for the inventor of the wheel to patent his invention and to chisel out of granite the few wheels that he could find the time for between hunting mammoths or fleeing from the odd sabre-toothed tiger. He would have needed to be a teacher as well as a doer. He is bound to have had some bright students who quickly grasped the principle of the new invention, but it is just as likely that he would have had some pretty slow students too, who had to have it drummed into them that a round wheel was infinitely superior to a square one and that it really was much more convenient to join the two front wheels together and the two back wheels together rather than to place the axles so as to link one front wheel with one back wheel on each side. And then there was the public. There is no reason to believe that people would have been any more open-minded then than they are now. So they would also have had to be educated. "If life without your so-called wheel was good enough for my father," some would have been saying, "then it's good enough for me."

Oh yes, there can be no doubt about it: teaching is the oldest profession of them all. In the beginning, it is clear, teaching and doing went hand-in-hand, and the first teachers were doers too. But as time went by specialisation reared its ugly head and the adage arose: "If you can, do; if you can't, teach." But what happens if a person can neither do nor teach? We have all experienced the result: incompetence, whether in a doer or a teacher.

When my father was a medical student in Germany before the Second World War, full professors were the only university teachers who were paid a salary. Everyone else had to rely on the fees that they received directly from those students who attended their lectures. This box-office system meant that every university teacher was in competition with every other in the same subject. As in any genuine free-market

economy, the dominant forces were demand and supply. Each
lecturer could offer a course on whatever he liked, even if it
duplicated a course given by one of his colleagues. He could
even schedule it at the same time as his rival's lectures if he
felt that would be to his advantage. My father, in fact, enrolled
for a course in Forensic Medicine given by a non-professorial
lecturer at exactly the same time and covering exactly the
same ground as the "official" course of lectures by the distinguished Professor of Forensic Medicine, who lectured to a
sparsely populated hall while his junior colleague's lectures
were full to overflowing. And it was not that the professor
was a bad lecturer but merely that his rival was better.

In Oxford and Cambridge there are still a few vestiges left
of a similar free enterprise system, though college porters are
no longer to be seen standing at the entrance to lecture halls
in order to collect fees. But in most universities and colleges
around the world competition has disappeared altogether, if
it ever existed, to be replaced by a centralised system in which
some committee, caucus or individual decides who is to teach
what, when, where – and sometimes even how.

This modern arrangement is of course tailor-made for
mediocrity. Each lecturer, no matter how incompetent, now
has a monopoly of his own little enclave without fear of competition from anyone else. At any rate, there is no *direct*
competition. But even indirect competition – the informal
comparisons students draw between their different lecturers
– can be controlled to some extent. What happens, in the
more extreme cases where mediocrity fears comparison with
brilliance, is that the mediocrity who controls the allocation
of lecture topics simply makes sure that his abler rival is
shunted out into teaching some obscure and unimportant section of the syllabus, while he himself hogs the central and
popular areas. This is rather more easily achieved than might
be thought, as mediocrities are much more likely than their
abler rivals to have the time-or temperament for inveigling
their way on to key committees.

This all boils down to bad news for you, the student. What
can you do about it? It will probably be very difficult for you
to get rid of a bad teacher unless, besides his incompetence,
he can be proved to be Jack the Ripper in drag, or worse.
Always remember that teaching ability tends to be fairly low
down on the list of priorities before a selection committee.
In the days when appointments could virtually be made

singlehandedly by an all-powerful professor whose word was law, there was, paradoxically, a better chance that ability would be recognised and rewarded. Having sole responsibility for his department as well as complete power over it, he would take great pride in it, knowing that his own reputation would be a reflection of that of his team. And so he would select the best team that he could find. But the "democratisation" of the power-structure of universities has resulted in appointments being made by committees, whose lowest common denominator is almost invariably mediocrity. Instead of pride, the ruling passion has become fear – the fear of each individual mediocrity that he might be overshadowed by the new appointee. And a gifted teacher is as much to be feared as a brilliant researcher – indeed, more so, as his ability will be more quickly recognised and more greatly appreciated by the student population.

A prudent course of action has therefore to be adopted. First, evaluate your lecturers. There are several clearly discernible types. Then react accordingly. There will always be some lecturers who are difficult to classify, but the problem will rarely be insoluble. These tricky cases will generally be hybrids of two or more types and should be treated according to the proportion of each type that they display. There are five main types, and we shall take them one by one.

The reader

Seven or eight hundred years ago, when the universities of Europe were in their infancy, someone who came before an audience of students and read out aloud to them the contents of a book was doing them an inestimable service, one which they could not easily do for themselves. Books in those days, before the invention of printing, were laboriously hand-copied by monks, and therefore very scarce and very expensive. Needless to say, libraries were small, with each book securely chained to its shelf. There might be literally only one or two manuscripts of a particular work in the whole world. In the absence of catalogues, let alone of the modern electronic paraphernalia which we now take so much for granted, tracing the whereabouts of a specific book might take years, not to mention the time actually spent in travelling to see it. The scholar who addressed an audience in, say, Oxford, might well have spent half a lifetime visiting Paris, Bologna, Heidelberg and Prague in order to assemble his material. Just reading aloud extracts from this priceless store of information of his was enough to earn him the undying gratitude of his hearers. Such were the earliest "lectures", a word coming from a Latin root signifying a "reading" (though the term "reader" came later on to be used for a higher rank of lecturer).

Old habits die hard. Today, five and a half centuries after the advent of the printing press, there are still a good number of university lecturers who act as if they have never heard of Gutenberg's little invention and who remain "lecturers" in the strictly literal sense. Most of them do not read straight out of a book, as that would be a little too obvious. In one case of which I know, the lecturer in question had had the standard textbook – or at least large chunks of it – typed up on loose sheets, which were duly punched and inserted into a ring binder. The "lectures" consisted of reading aloud from this impressive sheaf of "notes". The stupidity of such an attempt at deception amazes me even more than the incompetence it reveals, for the moment a student opened the textbook and began to use it in conjunction with his lecture notes he would be bound to notice an uncanny resemblance between the two. A subtler approach, which is more frequently encountered, is for the lecturer to rely not upon any of the prescribed textbooks but on one which he has been careful *not* to mention to his students, and which therefore only an exceptionally adventurous spirit would be likely to discover in the interstices of some library basement stack.

If you copy from one book, it has been said, you are guilty of plagiarism; if you copy from half a dozen books, that is research. The average lecturer is generally well aware of this fine dividing line and most are therefore careful in preparing their lectures to avoid relying too exclusively on a single book. The typical set of lecture notes will be compiled from several sources, some perhaps extensively copied and others merely paraphrased. The whole compilation is then either typed or written out in longhand into a notebook or file, from where it is ceremoniously read out aloud in instalments to the assembled student victims.

You may well be wondering what could possibly be wrong with this. Are you not, after all, getting a carefully prepared set of notes? Why should you mind if bits of it – or, for that matter, the whole lot – have been lifted straight out of the textbook? All the better, surely, as you may then be saved the bother of having to read the textbook yourself!

If the whole series of lectures is read out at dictation speed, as some obliging lecturers do, sometimes even with every comma called out aloud, then you may possibly be right, depending on how good the lecturer's notes were to begin with. As an undergraduate I attended the lectures of a brilliant professor, a truly original mind, who unfortunately had a very bad stutter. It was probably for this reason that he tended to read his lectures from his notes. Whenever he reached a word which he could not pronounce (especially a word starting with a "c" or a "p") he would feel obliged to go back to the beginning of the sentence and start again, in order, I always used to think, to take a sort of running jump at the troublesome word. This of course slowed him down considerably, so that it was quite easy to take down every word he said. The notes that I came away with were pure gold, for, unlike the usual "reader", this professor had not merely transcribed or even paraphrased the work of others: his notes were a product of his own fine intelligence. But I also found that I did not really have to listen to what he was saying in order to take notes. My mind would wander freely and I would not even know at the end of a lecture what topic it had been on. But, lo and behold, there in my notebook was a verbatim record of everything that he had said. I had become a mere writing machine during his lectures, allowing the boring voice droning on in the background to dictate directly to my hand without really going through my brain.

In short, despite the excellence of the notes, this professor's lectures were literally a waste of time. Had his notes been conveniently typed out and offered for sale, or available in published form, I would have been spared the endless tedium of many wasted hours. But, like his less gifted fellow "readers", this brilliant academic clearly did not recognise the vast difference between the spoken and the written word.

Many years later, when I myself was already a professor and a head of department, I was amused to hear a member of my staff airily informing all and sundry in a voice of great authority how one could tell whether someone was or was not a good lecturer. All you had to do, he said, was to look at the person's lecture notes. The quality of the notes would immediately indicate the calibre of the lecturer. My staff member obviously did not realise how revealing a remark that was, as it only proved how poor a lecturer he himself was!

The point is that if a person wants to convey information,

concepts or ideas by word of mouth he has to adopt a very different approach from the one required in order to communicate in writing. When something is written down the reader can go over it as many times as he likes. But in a speech or lecture it is essential for the speaker to carry his audience with him as he proceeds, so a certain amount of judicious repetition is normally necessary for comprehension as well as for emphasis.

Secondly, no matter how hard one tries to avoid it, written English is always just that bit more formal, more distant, than spoken English. It is partly a matter of vocabulary, partly a question of idiom and partly a function of grammar. In colloquial speech, sentences tend to be shorter, more pointed and direct than they are in writing, and sometimes expressive phrases are used which are not full sentences at all – not to mention gestures and facial expressions, any one of which may convey more than pages of dull print. All this helps to make the spoken word more readily understood by an audience than the read-aloud written word.

Once the speaker has lost his audience the communication is at an end and he is essentially talking to himself. This is especially true in the case of lectures on difficult concepts, and above all where it is impossible to understand a concept without grasping the one that went before, as in most mathematical and scientific subjects. And, unless you can literally take down every word, symbol or term, any notes you take after losing the lecturer's train of thought will be of no use to you. Students often carry on regardless, persuading themselves that the notes they take will be bound to make sense once they have a chance to go over them in the privacy of their boudoir. But if you have not really understood what the lecturer was on about this is a forlorn hope.

One of the chief problems with "readers" is that their lectures, couched as they are in the written rather than the spoken language, are on the whole much harder to follow than lectures delivered more freely. That does not mean to say that the best lecturers are invariably those who speak without any notes at all. Such people are often performers, who regard giving a lecture as a kind of circus act. They therefore perform feats of memory by reeling off whole lists of names or other equally meaningless information, simply in order to show off. Or, what is worse, they may be essentially lazy people who try to "wing" their way through a topic on which they are inadequately prepared. But, even if they know their stuff, the lack of guidance from notes of any kind may well result in their lectures being poorly organised, unstructured and, as a result, difficult to follow.

There is the story about the celebrated classicist who gave a much-acclaimed public lecture on Homer's *Iliad*. After he had finished, a member of his audience rushed up to him excitedly to express her appreciation and to ask him whether she could possibly borrow his notes. "With the greatest of pleasure, madam," replied the lecturer, reaching into his inside coat pocket and proffering a very scrunched up old envelope, on the back of which there were four words scribbled in pencil, two of which were the same: "Zeus, Agamemnon, Zeus, Achilles." These "notes" were sufficient to serve the professor as an outline of his lecture and, presumably, to prevent him from straying from his point.

In my experience the best lectures are usually given neither by "readers" nor by those who speak without any notes, but by lecturers whose notes, though usually fuller than those of the apocryphal classicist, do not amount to a complete text. Every second a speaker spends with his eyes glued to his notes is a second of lost eye-contact with his audience.

Have you ever tried carrying on a conversation with someone whose back was turned? It is for this reason that eye-contact is so important. Without it there can be no rapport between speaker and audience. With it, not only can a lecturer tell whether his audience is hanging rapt on his every word, dozing off on him or walking out of the door, but the experienced speaker can also quickly discern the more elusive qualities of puzzlement, boredom, irritation, annoyance and plain old-fashioned stupefaction chiselled on his hearers' features.

What can you do about it all? If attendance at lectures is compulsory, not very much. Of course, you may wonder why an institution should bother to insist upon attendance. After all, if the lectures were worthwhile, would most students not attend voluntarily in any case? More productively, you may do what I did when I had to attend the really useless lectures of a lacklustre "reader" whose notes were heavily dependent upon the standard textbook. The textbook was stodgy and old-fashioned enough, containing as it did a great deal of factual information with very little by way of interpretation or insights of any kind. But the lacklustre lecturer's rendition of it was positively excruciating. What I did was to bring the textbook with me to each lecture, keep it open at the appropriate place and, sitting under his nose, follow his mindless reading with my finger. On the extremely rare occasions when anything was added to the textbook's account, I would jot it down in the margin, these marginalia being the only notes I ever took in his lectures. Needless to say, this practice did not exactly endear me to my dreary lecturer, though it did save me a good deal of paper.

Of course, where such totally profitless lectures are optional, you are best advised to cut them, especially if they not only repeat the textbook almost word for word but are also delivered in so dull and monotonous a way as to send your mind scurrying to another world. But there is one important caveat.

Be sure to find out well in advance whether your boring lecturer is going to be setting the examination at the end of the year. If so, it is generally best to grit your teeth and go to his lectures, even if attendance is not compulsory. Academics are notorious prima donnas and, believe it or not, some *will* notice your absence – yes, even in a class of a hundred and fifty – and take it as a personal affront. Also, no printed syllabus can ever be as specific as a course of lectures. The published syllabus will give you a list of topics to be covered but will not asterisk the ones that the examiner is particularly fond of. Even past examination papers can be misleading here, especially if there has been a change of examiners. No matter how bad, the examiner's own course of lectures cannot but give you a clue as to his predilections and favoured approaches. Of course, if your examiner is a sadist he may deliberately mislead you and concentrate his lecturing efforts on those areas of the syllabus which he is planning to omit from the examination paper. But by that time you should have got to know him well enough to realise this.

In short, the lecturer is quite as important as his lectures. In the case of the "reader" whose lectures are not themselves of any value, discovering the emphasis, preferences and personality of the lecturer is the *only* reason for attending his lectures. However derivative his material may be, it is vital to find out where it comes from. Not necessarily the exact chapter and verse, though such information certainly can have its uses, but above all the *school* to which he adheres. Unoriginal minds almost invariably belong to one or other identifiable school of thought in their subject, unless they adopt the kindergarten approach of merely rattling off factual information and asking for it back in the examination – something which seems to happen most frequently in historical subjects and in the biological and medical sciences.

There are very few subjects which, if treated at anything approaching a true university level, are really cut-and-dried. A good lecturer will normally make his own position clear, though not without an exposition and critical assessment of views or interpretations with which he disagrees. It is usually more difficult to determine where your typical "reader" stands. With his tendency to lecture straight out of some standard textbook, his lectures may give the impression of impartiality – an impression which is likely to be belied by the way he marks your examination script. You have to be on the look-out for the odd tell-tale sign: tone of voice, the occasional parenthetical throw-away remark, even the rare raised eyebrow or hint of a frown. Be careful, however, not to over-react. What you take to be a significant clue to his secret thoughts may be merely a symptom of a nervous tic!

The pedant

When my dog Gaddy, a decidedly elderly bitch of indeterminate breed, suddenly gave birth to a litter of four, danger signalled. Before the puppies were old enough for their battery of vaccinations they were all stricken down by the deadly "parvo" virus, a close relation to the dread cat 'flu. The two males quickly succumbed, and their sisters had to pay repeated visits to the vet before they eventually got better. When their recovery was assured, the vet on duty, a youngish woman, told me that they would have to be vaccinated against the disease or they might catch it again. "But doesn't one attack of the virus confer lifelong immunity?" I enquired. My tone was confident, as this fact had been given to me by the young woman's employer, a more senior and experienced vet. To my surprise, however, she denied it, and when told the source of my information insisted that I must have misunderstood what had been said.

The young vet's mistake was a serious one. She clearly had no grasp of the basic nature of a viral infection or of vaccination. When Edward Jenner first introduced vaccination about two hundred years ago it had been known for centuries that a second attack of (viral) diseases such as smallpox or measles was extremely rare. It was this fact that gave Jenner the idea of preventing what could easily be a fatal attack of smallpox by infecting the patient with what was really a mini-attack of the disease (or, actually, of a closely related disease, cowpox). The success of vaccination in general is therefore based on the very fact that this vet was intent on denying: namely, that one attack of a viral disease usually safeguards the victim against a repetition.

Why should a qualified vet be so ignorant? It is not for me to say whether it was her fault or the fault of her teachers. But, even if their teaching was impeccable, we would still have to ask how someone with so complete a lack of understanding of something so fundamental could have been permitted to qualify in the first place. And, regardless of where the blame lies in this particular case, this kind of ignorance – an ignorance not of fact but of basic principle – is a typical result of pedantry.

In essence pedantry is the inability to see the wood for the trees. The pedant has no set of priorities: everything is equally important to him. Extreme pedants actually have an inverted set of priorities: the more trivial a piece of information is, the more important it is to them. And, above all, facts are more important to them than theories, principles or interpretations. So, in an extreme case, the number of buttons on King Louis XVI's coat would take precedence over an understanding of the causes of the French Revolution.

A pedant is one of the easiest of specimens to recognise. His pedantry is so integral a part of his personality that it shines through in everything he does. His manner of speech is often a dead give-away. He will never use a monosyllabic word if a sesquipedalian term would do just as well. He eschews colloquialisms of any kind and may affect a "posh" accent (though possibly lapsing into the vernacular when off guard). He may insist upon using such euphemisms as "perspiration" for "sweat", "perfume" for "scent", or "pass on" (or alternatively, "pass away") for "die". And, in his flight from "common" speech he is likely to fall into the error of over-correction by sounding the "t" in "often" and using "I" instead of "me", as in: "It will give my wife and I great pleasure" – a really bad solecism. I once had a schoolmaster who was so anxious to diguise his north-country accent that he took over-correction beyond the limit and would even pronounce "cushion" to rhyme with "Russian"!

Such curiosities of speech are harmless enough. In themselves they are perhaps worthy of a titter, if that. But they are also symptomatic of a much more deep-seated character trait. The pedant is essentially an insecure person. He tends to lack a sense of self-esteem – and, as a rule, not without good reason! Never a deep thinker, he clings to superficialities for dear life. They are his only claim to an individual identity. His pedantry is at once an attempt to impress others and to reassure himself.

As an examiner I recently had a typical pedant foisted upon me as external examiner. The type of question I like to set is open-ended, often based on a quotation, whether real or made-up, something like: "'Oliver Cromwell was a dictator.' Discuss." My external examiner was not happy with this sort of thing and wanted it to be rephrased as: "'Oliver Cromwell was a dictator.' Discuss this quotation by (?), with reference to the primary and secondary sources which you have studied." The unoriginal pedantic mind assumes that the quotation must have been taken from some "authority", whereas it was in fact merely a spoof quotation made up for the occasion by myself. As for the additional instructions, they can do no harm but are simply redundant, spelling out the obvious and thereby lowering the tone of a university honours examination to kindergarten level.

As a lecturer the pedant will be unoriginal, boring, finicky and shallow, adopting a cut-and-dried approach to even the most interesting and controversial of subjects. If he is also to be your examiner, beware. He will expect you to be as petty-minded as himself. Omit some small detail that *he* considers vital and you are for the high-jump. Introduce your own interpretation and you are dead. So, if you have identified your lecturer-examiner as a pedant, make sure you know *exactly* what his likes and dislikes are. Pedants are not famous for their tolerance.

But if your pedantic lecturer is *not* going to examine you, you may be in an even worse plight. If he is isolated, with his colleagues adopting a very different, non-pedantic, approach, you may as well stop going to his lectures. It will also be necessary, however, to find out more precisely what your examiner's tendencies and predilections are. It is a safer bet, though, that, even if your pedantic lecturer does not set the examination, your examiner will be a pedant too. This is especially likely in certain subjects where pedantry has gained a foothold, one of them, alas, being history, where pedantry and Marxism – just another kind of intellectual strait-jacket – are about equally strong.

"Every historical fact is concrete and unique" is a formula which I first heard uttered by a world-famous Cambridge history professor. It has since become a sort of battle-cry trotted out whenever necessary to combat the supposedly dangerous view that one can actually use the past to predict the future. Obviously, if every historical fact is unique this cannot be done. If something is "unique" there is no other exactly like it, and if no two facts are exactly alike, no parallels may be drawn and no conclusions extrapolated from one situation to another. This robs the study of history of any useful social function, but this lowering of sights does not upset very many historians. On the contrary, the sighs of relief have been almost audible.

The point is that in order to "apply" historical knowledge to the present or future a comparative approach has to be adopted. This necessitates the study of, not one but at least two and preferably more, quite different eras and societies. What is more, it will not be enough to assemble information. For useful comparisons to be drawn there will have to be a good deal of analysis, interpretation and really deep thinking – something which straightaway offends against the pedantic mentality.

It is generally believed that depth and breadth are opposites: the more you have of the one, the less of the other. This is true enough in regard, say, to the digging of a hole in the ground. You may either dig a deep and narrow hole or a broad and shallow one and obtain roughly the same amount of earth. But it doesn't apply to intellectual pursuits, where it is often necessary to have breadth – as in making comparisons – *precisely in order* to achieve depth.

The pedant is happy to rely on this "depth vs. breadth" fallacy. Not knowing the meaning of "depth" he is happy to equate it with narrowness, because in his mind both are the opposite of breadth. And by concentrating so narrowly on his own little speck of intellectual territory he can lay claim to that proudest of all current academic titles, that of "specialist". But it is worth remembering the old definition of that word: "A specialist is someone who knows more and more about less and less until he knows everything about nothing."

No wonder the pedants' chorus quickly took up the refrain, "Every historical fact is concrete and unique", which, besides being a cop-out, happens to be demonstrably untenable. The only way to find out whether every historical fact is or is not unique is to examine *every single* historical fact that has happened since the beginning of time – clearly an impossible task. Even if it *were* possible to do this and even if it turned out that every fact really *was* unique, that would still not prove that it was impossible to apply the knowledge of the past to the future. After all, we know that no two human brains are exactly identical, no two hearts, livers or any other organs, yet that does not stop the medical profession from talking about "the brain", "the heart", "the liver". If medical textbooks dealt only with Joe Bloggs's heart and refused to extrapolate from it to anyone else's heart because his heart was "unique", there could be no science of medicine.

Law is another subject where pedantry thrives. In recent decades the forces of pedantry have been on the defensive, largely thanks to the efforts of Lord Denning as Master of the Rolls, many of whose judgments (with certain notable exceptions) represent the interests of justice against the dictates of narrow literalism. One such case, *Re Rowland* (1963), involved mutual wills made by a young doctor and his wife just before going on holiday to the South Seas, where their boat was lost and they were both drowned. Each made a bequest in the event of the other's death "preceding or coinciding with my own death" – a form of words evidently designed to cover just such a contingency as actually occurred. In the Court of Appeal Lord Denning put forward this sensible view, but the majority held otherwise. The two deaths, they said, could not be proved to have "coincided" exactly in point of time, so the provisions of the wills were set aside! Needless to say, some of Lord Denning's doughtiest critics are to be found in the groves of Academe.

The indoctrinator

"I am accurate; you are biased; he is prejudiced." It is always the other chap whose view is slanted, never oneself. Yet, objectivity is practically impossible of attainment. No account can ever be complete, no matter what the subject-matter. By selecting some facts and omitting others, or even by emphasising some more than others, one is introducing one's own subjective viewpoint, whether deliberately or unintentionally.

This applies to every conceivable academic discipline. In a number of fields the battle-lines are drawn, and it is the easiest thing in the world for students to get caught in the crossfire. Economics has its monetarists, its neo-Keynesians and its Marxists, to mention but three; psychologists may belong to one of a dozen competing schools; and, though the party lines in other subjects may be less obvious, that does not mean they don't exist. It should not take too long to determine to which school your lecturer or tutor belongs. But what do you do if you happen to disagree with him? Do not make the mistake of assuming that he will tolerate dissent, even if his school of thought is one whose principles are love, liberty and universal brotherhood. Such people have a tendency of being the biggest hypocrites of all.

That is not to say that there are *no* tolerant academics, only that they are *very* few and far between. If you do happen to stumble upon one, know that you have found a rare gem. In disagreeing with a lecturer's pet theory, no matter how gently, you will have to feel your way very carefully. If you are absolutely certain that the teacher in question is not going to have the opportunity of cutting you down to size behind the scenes in the examination at the end of the year, go ahead and voice your dissent. But even then, beware: the chances are that his views will be shared by others, including those who mark your examination script. Of course, you may decide to express your own independent ideas during the course but toe the party line in the examination. On the whole, though, when in doubt it is advisable to be a chameleon: change colour to match the academic environment in which you find yourself and save your dissenting views for the day of your graduation, otherwise that day may never come!

The fuddy-duddy

University and college lecturers are seldom trained to teach. Some institutions offer the new appointee a short course designed to enable him to avoid the worst excesses of amateurism: a tendency to mumble into his beard even if he is clean-shaven or female; an irrepressible desire to confide his main points to the blackboard; or (mostly in the case of a woman, though not exclusively so) an unerring knack for choosing to wear the most pendulous earrings, whose rhythmic swaying first distracts the audience and then mesmerises them. Beyond such rudimentary instruction the average university or college teacher is left very much to fend for himself, and it is taken for granted that he *will* be able to teach his subject. He *does* have a degree in it, after all, if not several.

But there is something more elusive than the right stance to adopt or the best way to project one's voice, something probably even more important than the subject-matter of one's course. It is the intellectual and methodological approach adopted in lecturing – something which university and college lecturers are hardly ever taught. This is especially important in subjects needing a good deal of explanation, like mathematics, or where there are competing and mutually exclusive methods on the market, as in the elementary teaching of a language.

How then does a new appointee – or an old one, for that matter – decide what his method or approach is to be? In practice, most university teachers probably never even think about it. They just do what comes naturally – teach the subject the way *they* were taught. But, once they have taught it that way for a year or two there is a tendency amongst some of them to regard it as part of themselves. If anyone dares to criticise their method of teaching he criticises *them* – and to this type of personality nothing is more unacceptable than criticism.

Your typical – or should I say, archetypical – fuddy-duddy is someone who not only teaches by an outmoded method but who will also not brook any criticism of himself or it. It is an attitude which we might perhaps have expected in schoolteachers rather than in university or college lecturers, and it *is* true that it is particularly common amongst those who teach elementary subjects such as beginner's Latin and Greek, which, now that Classics has lost its pre-eminence in the school curriculum, are often offered by institutions of tertiary education.

I have encountered a surprising number of students who have told me that they "used to be" very good at Latin but that they subsequently had trouble coping with it. Their explanation is always the same: that they were good at grammar but could not manage translation. The reason for this is invariably that they were required to learn whole tables of paradigms (like the well-known "*amo, amas, amat . . .*") off by heart without understanding what it was all about. This was the "grammar" that they were supposedly good at, which only meant that they were able to reproduce the tables accurately. Not surprisingly, they had no idea how to apply this "grammar" to translating actual sentences. Hence their subsequent problems with the language.

The "advanced" methods of teaching Latin which are now prevalent go to the other extreme of shunning formal grammar altogether. In the hands of a fuddy-duddy teacher such a method can become quite lethal, as the teacher will then superimpose upon this avant-garde course the antediluvian approach to grammar that *he* was taught by. The resulting mixture can easily be explosive enough to destroy all learning, understanding and interest in the subject.

There is actually no reason why Latin should be such a bugbear. Unlike some esoteric subject such as philosophy or higher mathematics, the learning of a language is something that should be well within the intellectual grasp of any normal human being. After all, everyone can speak at least one language, and for a very long time Latin was spoken by millions of people every day. That is not to say it should be taught in the way infants learn their mother-tongue, but just because it is a dead language also does not mean it should be taught by a deadly method which could easily be mistaken for an ancient form of torture.

When I myself devised my own elementary Latin course for university students I found that I had to give all the lectures myself, even though I was already a full professor by then. I had started by asking a junior lecturer to take half the class, but before long the students of that group complained. One of the features of my course was the active teaching of Latin vocabulary by means of English derivatives. The students were asked to enter all new words in a vocabulary book ruled into three columns. Each new Latin word was entered in the left-hand column and its English equivalents in the right-hand column. Between these two columns was the column in which the derivatives appeared, which therefore could be used as a stepping-stone from the Latin word in column one to its English translation in column three. Thus, for example, the Latin word *miles*, *militis* would be entered on the left-hand side. What would appear in the middle column were English derivatives from it such as the word "military". With these two columns filled in, the third column could easily be worked out: *miles* must mean "soldier". In short, it is an approach

to vocabulary which avoids the necessity of learning the mean-
ings off by heart. And it also has the additional advantages
of being intrinsically interesting and helping to expand the
students' English vocabulary. But my assistant evidently did
not understand this approach to vocabulary and, being a
devotee of the cult of rote memorisation, got the students to
enter the derivatives not in the middle column, where they
could be used as a stepping-stone to the meaning, but in the
third column on the extreme right. The result of this arrangement and the whole approach adopted by my assistant was
that, for the students in that half of the class, far from being
a useful aid, the derivatives came to be seen as just another
column to be learnt off by heart – exactly the opposite of
what was intended!

The trouble is that students very rarely know anything about
methodology. They will normally assume that the way they
are being taught the subject, no matter what it is, is the way
to teach it. If you find you can understand the subject all
right and are making good progress, there is probably no
need to query the method. But if you making heavy weather
of it, it may well be because you have a fuddy-duddy lecturer
who is teaching by an archaic method. If so, you should seek
help. A fresher and livelier approach to the subject may make
all the difference, and it may be worth it even if you have to
pay for private lessons.

The Socratic guide

A late great-aunt of mine was in the habit of saying that
everything in life was either a matter of taste or a matter of
opinion. This remark of hers is perhaps a bit too sweeping,
but it is undoubtedly very relevant to the question of how
you judge the merits of a university teacher. A pedantic student (and there is certainly no shortage of them), himself
destined to become a pedantic university teacher, is quite
likely to single out for emulation a pedantic teacher of his
own. One such fledgling pedant-cum-fuddy-duddy once even
went so far as to attack me in an anonymous letter to the
student newspaper when I described myself on the title-page
of one of my books as Ph.D. (Cambridge) instead of by the
more conventional designation of Ph.D. (Cantab), which my
critic in his wisdom assumed was the only correct form. What
he did not know was that the Latin "Cantabrigia" (or its
adjective, "Cantabrigiensis", of which "Cantab" is an abbrevi-

ation), was actually derived from the English form, "Cambridge", and not *vice versa*. All that "Cambridge" means is of course the bridge over the river Cam, whereas "Cantabrigia" has no meaning at all.

One of the most famous teachers of all time was Socrates, who never gave a formal lecture but employed a question-and-answer dialectic, the so-called "Socratic method". Socrates recognised what is probably one of the great truths about the relationship between teaching and learning: that the most effective teacher is not the one who pushes his students in the direction in which he wants them to go but the one who can manage to guide his students' tottering footsteps in order to enable them to direct their own course. It was this view of education which was expressed by one of my own lecturers, who would begin his first-year course of lectures each year with these words: "Ladies and gentlemen, I am not here to teach you History; I am here to teach you how to teach yourselves History." This goal can seldom be achieved by means of formal lectures alone, and most universities and colleges therefore supplement them with tutorials, a more "Socratic" mode of teaching.

Tutorials

There is an apocryphal Oxford story about a freshman undergraduate whose tutor asks him which lectures he plans to attend. He enthusiastically hands his tutor a timetable with numerous blocks filled in. But the comment is not reassuring. The tutor peers at him over his bifocal lenses. "Smithers," he says, "I thought you came here to do some *work*." The clear implication is that attending lectures is not "work" but, presumably, play.

But, despite this, a really outstanding lecture can sometimes be as valuable as a good tutorial, and a bad tutorial can easily degenerate into an equally poor lecture. I once had the misfortune to have a tutor who, though I was his only student, would read to me from his notes as if he was lecturing (badly) to a class of fifty. Conversely, it is possible to have a certain amount of give and take and some genuine discussion in a lecture. I have attempted this – with some success, I believe – even in a lecture of over 350 students. I would have before me a photograph of everyone in the class and I would call on individuals by names. Though only a few could participate each time, everyone would have to be on his toes every time as he would not know when it would be his turn.

It is commonly supposed that the ideal tutorial group is one person, but as a Cambridge don I always preferred to teach pairs or even groups of three rather than individuals. This permitted some exchange between the students themselves as well as between each student and myself.

But, despite the high reputation which the tutorial system still enjoys, it does not always work as well in practice as it is meant to. Even in Oxbridge, there have always been many instances of less than satisfactory tutorials or (as they are called in Cambridge) supervisions.

The time-honoured practice of having the undergraduate read his weekly essay aloud is wasteful in the extreme. Even if the tutor does not doze off during this ritual and even if he actually jots the odd note on the back of a cigarette-box to remind him of points he wishes to take up afterwards, the plain fact of the matter is that by the time the ceremonial reading is over nearly half the tutorial time has gone. In my experience the average tutorial essay takes about twenty minutes to read out aloud. The really bad tutor actually welcomes this, as there is then less time left for him to make a fool of himself in. Not that all tutorials run for a full hour in any case. And even some good tutors sometimes just don't give value for money. A well-known and much-beloved Cambridge don of my acquaintance, for example, would sometimes send his "supervisee" (to use an awful Cambridge neologism) away with nothing more than a brief and cryptic comment, and one which was not always repeatable. The poor undergraduate who had spent days working on an essay on the Battle of Waterloo would finish reading his masterpiece aloud only to be greeted by a pregnant pause during which his supervisor would puff a good few times slowly and sagely on his ever-present pipe. Then finally would come the sole comment: "Funny buggers those Froggies." The student who happened to have his supervision at eleven o'clock in the morning would get a less relevant remark, coupled with a yawn: "Never make love in the morning."

Students also often prefer to read their essays to their tutor as the time-honoured ritual will generally give them an extra day or two in which to do the work – an important consideration to a hard-pressed undergraduate but a very short-term advantage. If the essay is handed in in advance, not only can the whole hour be devoted to discussion but there is also no excuse for the tutor's not having scrutinised the essay carefully. So, ultimately the student will be the beneficiary.

Even if your tutor is a staunch upholder of the time-honoured essay-reading routine, let him have your essay at least 24 hours, and preferably two days, in advance, and see what happens. If that does not do the trick and he hands you your essay back unread at the beginning of the tutorial, you could tell him that you develop the most frightful stutter whenever you have to read anything aloud. Tell him whatever you like, but try to persuade him to mark the essay before the tutorial and not to waste your time and money – for that is what it is even if it's being paid for by a state grant.

Or, if all else fails and you still have to read your essay out aloud, try to persuade your tutor to interrupt you whenever he has a point to make. Despite the trauma, this is usually much more profitable than waiting until the bitter end, by which time the chances are that he will have forgotten what he wanted to say.

The reading-aloud tutorial ritual, so far as I know, is very much confined to Oxford and Cambridge, and even there it is less in evidence today than it used to be. But, strangely enough, it has crept in in other institutions in a new guise: that of the "class" or "seminar", which is now almost as commonly found in undergraduate as in postgraduate education. Each meeting revolves around a student "paper" – usually a much longer and more elaborate document than the average tutorial essay – which is read to the assembled group, generally a mix of students and academics. Sometimes the paper is duplicated and circulated in advance, which saves a lot of time and cuts out the tedium of the reading ritual – except that most group members will not have read it and the discussion will suffer as a result. In principle the seminar is an excellent idea. The informality, the encouragement of discussion, the interspersing of young with old, students with academics, and, where it occurs, the straddling of the boundaries between disciplines, are all very commendable. But it often proves a much less valuable educational vehicle than might have been hoped or expected. The presence of a number of academics sometimes unfortunately leads to their talking to one another and rather shutting out the students, especially undergradates. There is also a regrettable tendency for seminar papers to focus on narrow topics with which only a small minority of those present are likely to be familiar.

One problem that is unlikely to occur in a seminar, especially in the presence of a number of senior members, is one which plagues especially the bigger tutorial groups prevalent in universities outside Oxford and Cambridge, and that is the temptation for the tutor to turn his tutorials into lectures. I use the word "temptation" advisedly, because it is actually much easier to deliver a passable lecture than to give an effective tutorial. In a lecture there is no need for two-way communication, and most lectures are in fact monologues – though the very best lectures never are. But one of the great strengths of the tutorial system is the opportunities it creates for interaction. By their very nature, tutorials are much more unstructured than lectures. It is impossible for a tutor to plan everything that he is to say in his tutorial in the way that a lecturer often does. The discussion may take unexpected twists and turns, and questions may arise which the tutor has never thought about before. These are healthy signs, indications that the tutorial system is really working.

But in order for it to succeed the tutor must not be afraid, hoping against hope at every turn that he *will* be able to field the questions which come his way. Once anxiety creeps in, the whole atmosphere changes to that of a lions' den, with a terrified tutor holding the wild animals at bay with a chair. It is perhaps the subconscious fear that such a situation may arise that makes so many tutors take the easy way out and allow their tutorials to degenerate into monologues. And the students are usually equally to blame, as they too are often apprehensive about being picked upon and having questions fired at them in the presence of their peers. Most would much rather sit there passively pen in hand taking down the "gospel" being imparted to them from on high.

Do not allow yourself to be short-changed. A true tutorial system, though it may place you under pressure and possibly even cause you embarrassment at times, is far more beneficial to you than anything else. Dialogue will help the tutorial to become an informal discussion session in which thoughts are exchanged and ideas forged on the anvil of logic, which is surely the ideal of the tutorial system. And it is not just the interaction between teacher and taught that is valuable, but also the interaction between student and student, where that occurs.

I once knew a university teacher who was often to be seen walking out of his own tutorial after the first few minutes.

This was a deliberate technique of his which was designed, as he put it, "to allow the young to speak more freely". Needless to say, it did not work. Left to themselves without a tutor the students had no guidance, not only on the substantive issues before them but also, which is hardly less important, on the approach to the writing of their essays.

This vital task of the tutorial often receives less attention than it deserves, even when the tutor is not absent. The ability to tackle a problem-type essay-question is one of the most important and practical skills to be learnt from a university education. The actual subject that a student reads for his degree often turns out to be of no real value to him in his working life, but there are few occupations which do not require some writing skills. But, even without taking so long-term a view, where is a student to learn the techniques he needs for his course of study if not in tutorials? A lecture is an inappropriate vehicle for teaching how, for example, to handle a gobbet question, that age-old bane of the life of the student of the humanities (see page 130). That is a task for which the tutorial format is tailor-made. The chief beauty of the tutorial, in fact, is its flexibility, its adaptability to suit the needs of the individual student – each and every individual student. Unfortunately, tutors are often not as skilful as they ought to be, one of the reasons for this being the low-grade label that most universities stick on tutorials – and on tutors. But, now that you know what you are entitled to expect, if you are not getting as much out of your tutorials as you feel you should, don't be shy to ask.

CHAPTER III

HITLER'S HEIRS

Every employee tends to rise to his level of incompetence.
— *Laurence J Peter*

When I was a student at Cambridge I was something of a politico. Among other things, I was college NUS secretary, which, besides a number of more mundane chores, entailed going twice a year to the conferences of the National Union of Students, the venue for which alternated between a university city and out-of-season Margate, a bleak and windswept ghost-town. At one such conference I immediately noticed the absence of the president of the students' union of another university, whom I had got to know quite well from previous conferences. When I asked a member of his university's delegation why my friend was not present I received a rather strange reply. Looking furtively around him as if he was afraid of being overheard, my informant whispered conspiratorially: "He shook hands with the Queen." It occurred to me that it was bad form to shake hands with the Queen instead of bowing. But could that possibly be the reason for my friend's disgrace? In fact, what had happened was that when the Queen visited my friend's university the radical students' union decided to boycott her visit. My friend, though president of the union, was a little less radical than his colleagues and deigned to greet the royal visitor instead of ignoring her presence.

This episode only underlines the unreality of a good deal of university politics – of the senior no less than of the student variety. The highest degree of senselessness is attained when the two come together. I remember, for example, when I was secretary of the Cambridge Student Representative Council, as it was then called, at a time when student radicalism was sweeping through the campuses of American and continental universities. In Britain, and especially in Cambridge, the "student revolution" was a very tame affair indeed, yet I was amused to see the way in which certain highly placed university authorities bowed to every breeze, no matter how slight, that they detected blowing in a radical direction.

Academic politicians are not exactly notorious for their vision, but the over-reaction which I witnessed was at least honest, though I did not realise at the time how rare a quality

46

that is. One of the biggest problems is the tendency for academics to give up their purely academic pursuits and to begin to pursue power instead, on a full-time basis. The traditional Oxbridge pattern – now, alas, on the wane even there – encouraged dons to combine administrative posts with teaching and research. Not too long ago the full-time academic bureaucrat was virtually a non-existent species. Even heads of colleges, with the very considerable administrative responsibility that such a position entails, found the time to continue with their academic work at the same time. When I was a Cambridge don, the Master of my college, one of the largest colleges in that university, used to visit the Public Record Office in London two or three times a week in order to do his research, and it was during his mastership that he produced some of the most important – and voluminous – academic work of his distinguished career. Not that his administrative work in the college suffered in any way. He was conscientious to a fault and attended to his duties as head of house with an exemplary dedication coupled with an enviable sense of balance and perspective, and, not least, without the slightest trace of arrogance or self-importance.

Ex-academics and dys-academics
But his is a dying breed, one which has long been extinct in a number of universities around the world. Instead, the move is towards the concentration of power in the hands of a small group – in some cases better described as a clique – of what can only be called ex-academics, people who have given up positions as university teachers to become full-time bureaucrats. Students are sometimes baffled by this phenomenon – and rightly so. What sort of academic would wish to become a mere pen-pusher?

The answer is an ambitious one, a power-seeker. But that in itself is not enough to make this type of character so sinister. Most people, after all, seek power of one sort or another in one way or another. No, the real problem is that bureaucratic positions in educational institutions offer a ready-made escape-hatch for the academic cripple: the incompetent lecturer, the non-writing professor, the mediocre mind. If such a person, not only an ex-academic but also what we might call a "dys-academic", holds sway over real academics, it does not take any great powers of the imagination to realise what is likely to happen. And if you throw in a measure or two of

good old-fashioned envy on the part of the dys-academic viewing the true academic, the mixture could easily become
explosive.*

How does all this affect you, the student? In a myriad
different ways, most of them hidden from view. Clashes will
be very likely to occur between the different echelons in your
university or college, especially if it is run by full-time ex-
academic bureaucrats. The outcome of such a conflict could
easily determine who your lecturers and tutors are to be, what
they will teach you, how you will be examined and, not least,
how well you will do.

If you ever have any dealings with a college or university
head or dean of any kind, it will repay you to do a little
research into his background. If he has practically no publications to his credit, beware. If, in addition, he does not possess
a Ph.D. or doctorate of any kind, take cover. The chances
are that you are in the presence of someone who has no real
interest in things academic and no real concern for your welfare. He is probably a wire-puller and a political manipulator.

Why, you may well ask, should a person's lack of publications and a doctorate be so incriminating? Or what is there
in the writing of academic treatises that makes their authors
saints? The short answer is: nothing at all. Those endowed
with doctorates and long publication lists are, unfortunately,
no more proof against deviousness, dishonesty and deceit
than those without such credentials. But a genuine academic
is less likely to harbour grudges born of envy – and he is also
less likely to be a bureaucrat in the first place, so he would
normally have less opportunity of indulging his prejudices
than the ex- or dys-academic.

Above all, the true academic is just a little more likely to
employ reason rather than political motivation in reaching
his conclusions. I once served on a selection committee for a
chair among the candidates for which was a man whose

---

* The author wishes to make it quite clear that he is *not* saying that *all*
full-time university administrators who happen to have given up their
academic work in order to devote themselves to university government
and administration are "dys-academics". There are indeed some very
distinguished academics whose scholarly fame is deservedly enormous
who have sought, or, more usually, been cajoled into accepting, that
sort of position. Such people stand out a mile, as a quick glance at their
publication lists will reveal, and there is no question of mistaking them
for "dys-academics".

academic record was anything but illustrious. In addition the committee happened to know that the candidate in question had deceived the institution concerned in regard to certain financial matters. And, as if all this was not enough to disqualify the candidate, he was also the subject of a positively damning report from one of the world's leading scholars in the field, who made it quite clear that he would not have the candidate as an ordinary lecturer in his department let alone recommend him for a professorship. Not suprisingly, the few genuine academics on the committee were unimpressed by the candidate's credentials, nor were they reassured by his showing at the interview. But they had not reckoned with the bureaucracy, which for its own reasons had determined that this was the man for the job. A spokesman for their interest quickly stepped into the breach. His chief object of attack was the damning report, whose tone was so extreme that, he opined, it could not but have been actuated by malice and had therefore to be totally disregarded. When the sheep – always the majority in any committee – saw which way the wind was blowing they duly followed suit and began bleating in unison.

But the bureaucracy does not have a monopoly of unreason. In fact, the mass of mankind are strangers to reasoned argument most of the time – and that includes the mass of university teachers. There are, however, one or two differences between the unreason of a clique of power-hungry bureaucrats and that of the rank and file of academic mediocrities. A ruthless bureaucracy is not only more resourceful in pursuing its aims but also more imaginative. By contrast, the means employed by the rank and file in furthering their own prejudices are negative: opposition to innovation; resentment of anything that resembles hard work; hostility to authority (except their own, of course); and, above all, fear of students.

Pseudo-arguments

As these irrational prejudices cannot be expressed openly, and as many of those who hold them will not even admit them to themselves, justification of them has to take the form of rationalisations couched as pseudo-arguments. One old favourite, already very much in evidence as long ago as 1908, when F.M. Cornford, a Cambridge don, wrote his tongue-in-cheek exposé of university politics, *Microcosmographica Academica*, is the proposition that *"The Time is not Ripe"*.

This pseudo-argument has a multitude of uses but is especially effective in resisting change of any kind. The beauty of it is that its protagonist does not have to oppose the innovation itself. On the contrary, he can wax lyrical in its praise. The only thing he has to urge is that *now* is not the time for it. As in the old story of the notice in the barber-shop, "Pay for your shave today and have a free shave tomorrow", tomorrow never comes. You can be quite sure that the time will *never* be ripe.

Now that students are increasingly represented on university committees and boards you may have the opportunity of encountering such pseudo-arguments at first hand. Do not make the (quite natural) mistake of taking them literally and trying to counter them as if they were genuine rational arguments. The best method of attack is to use one pseudo-argument to beat another. The appropriate one here would be the *"Agreement in Principle"* technique. This is normally used in order to shelve a proposal indefinitely: "I wholeheartedly agree *in principle* with Professor Bloggins's admirable proposal, but . . ." However, once something has been formally agreed upon in principle, it may just be possible to resuscitate it at a later date. So *"Agreement in Principle"* is at least one step up from *"the Time is not Ripe"* position.

Two closely related pseudo-arguments are the *"This has never been done before"* line and its exact opposite, *"This was tried ages ago and failed"*. Despite being contradictory and mutually exclusive, these are both rationalisations of the very same prejudice: once again, opposition to innovation. It should not take long to realise that the fact that something has not been done before is far from conclusive as an argument against it. Indeed, it should have more force as an argument in its favour. The logical conclusion of this pseudo-argument is of course, in Cornford's words, "that nothing should ever be done for the first time". But it has a remarkable appeal when addressed – as it almost invariably is – by fuddy-duddies to fuddy-duddies (see Chapter II for an explanation of the term).

The opposite position, "this was tried ages ago and failed", sounds much more persuasive. And so it should be – if true. However, those who favour this argument will not generally be found to be particularly scrupulous in the way they employ it. The similarity between the supposedly dangerous innovation which they wish to oppose and the one which they *allege* was tried unsuccessfully at some (usually indeterminate) date in the past will probably not stand up to scrutiny. Nor are these people always above simply inventing such a precedent, or even branding as a failure something which would more accurately be described as a signal success.

The rise of the mediocracy

All these pseudo-arguments are equally useful in combating another of the mediocrity's bugbears: fear of hard work. Changes of any kind, whether in the curriculum, the examination schedule or even the timetable, are likely to entail extra work for the lecturers or tutors involved: the preparation of new courses, not to mention the psychological wrench in parting with their yellowed and decaying notes; the unspeakable hardship of having to read a book or article or two for a change; and, above all, the agonising toil of putting pen to paper.

But there is also a smaller group of mediocrities who, far from shunning work, go out of their way to attract it. These are the most dangerous mediocrities of all. The kind of work they are so anxious to undertake invariably confers upon them a modicum of responsibility and, with it, power, though the tasks concerned are usually unglamorous in the extreme and therefore unattractive to the majority. A classic example is compiling the teaching timetable, an unenviable chore in most people's eyes. But our ambitious mediocrity is quick to volunteer for it, knowing that he now has the power to arrange everyone's teaching according to his own convenience. If he is devious (and he usually is), he can use this power as a bargaining chip: "I will give you the 10.30 slot if you give me . . ." Needless to say, this sort of deal is hardly ever expressed in so many words. Our over-eager climber is now poised to expand his empire. Taking on more and more administrative chores not only enhances his power and influence but also gives him a ready-made standing excuse for not finishing that Ph.D. thesis on which he has supposedly been working for the past twelve years or for not producing that book or article which he has been threatening to write for so long.

When I was a twelve-year-old schoolboy I found myself picked upon by a prefect on the grounds that my socks were drooping. There was a school rule that you had to wear garters, a rule which I had ignored. The prefect ordered me to write a five-page essay on the need to wear garters. When presented with an essay written in a sprawling hand on five of the smallest pages known to man, my persecutor saw red. It did not help matters that, as a doctor's son, I had devoted my essay not to a defence of garters but to attacking them as injurious to health and liable to stop the flow of blood to the extremities. I had of course obeyed the letter, if not the spirit, of the prefect's instruction. But, instead of accepting defeat gracefully, he was determined to teach me a lesson. It was then that I decided to go and see the acting headmaster, who speedily put a stop to my harassment.

It is very much the same type of self-serving vindictiveness – only less innocent – that one tends to find in the exercise of power by mediocrities in institutions of tertiary education. Such people have nothing better to do with their time than to victimise those beneath them, the students – or, to be more precise, those students who have occasioned the mediocrities' displeasure. This is most effectively done behind the scenes, by means of punitive marking, negative reports or even false tattle-taling. Seeing others squirm gives such people quite a kick, and their own self-esteem is generally so low that the only thing that can give them satisfaction is the discomfiture of those whom they dislike, the reason for their dislike generally being envy of what they (rightly, for once) perceive to be superiority to themselves.

The underlying motive in all this is fear – the fear of being exposed. The aggressive mediocrity, eagerly snapping up any opportunity to expand his power-base, turns out to be simply a more active – and more dangerous – twin brother of the work-shy variety. Both instinctively recognise their own mediocrity and are terrified of anyone who might unmask them – notably, therefore, of their own students. This fear is revealed in many ways, one of the more innocent of its manifestations being the keeping of a howler-book, as we saw in Chapter I (page 23). But, in whatever they do these weak personalities need to reassure themselves of their own superiority to their students.

It is for this reason that the "democratisation" of universities, which has been a feature of recent years, bodes ill for you, the student. Though there is now a certain amount of student representation on university bodies, it is for the most part only token representation. The real beneficiaries of "democratisation" are the lower echelons of university teachers, amongst whose ranks the fear-ridden mediocrities we have just been describing are likely to be dominant.

In my youthful run-in with the officious prefect the person in authority who came to my rescue was the second master, who was acting headmaster at the time, as the headmaster himself was away on long leave. It was just as well for me that he was. The headmaster, a thoroughly conventional and generally weak character, would almost certainly have acted like most people in authority and sided with the prefect. This is, after all, the path of least resistance. By comparison with a twelve-year-old first-former a prefect is a figure of authority. Whereas a first-former is a defenceless individual a prefect belongs to a powerful elite group, the other members of which can be expected to rally around him in full force. In supporting a prefect the headmaster is upholding the duly constituted authority and consecrated chain of command of his establishment.

Why then did the acting headmaster side with me against the prefect? He clearly recognised – probably instinctively – that though it would be easier to side with the prefect against me, it would serve his own interests better for him to slap the prefect down. His action made it clear that he was firmly in charge and that even the high and mighty prefects were subject to his authority, something of which they might need an occasional gentle reminder. Of course, my incident was trivial. But if the acting headmaster had repeatedly sided against the prefects in issue after issue, he would, whether consciously or not, have been threatening to undermine their position. Sooner or later there would have been bound to be a showdown, the outcome of which would have been determined by the allies which the two sides were able to muster. In short, what we have here is an example of a classic pattern of the struggle for power – what may, for want of a better term, be described as the "nutcracker suite".

The nutcracker suite

In any institution, no matter how democratic, there is always a hierarchy of power. In a university there are generally four echelons. The greatest amount of power is concentrated in the hands of a smallish group at the top made up of full-time and near-full-time bureaucrats (chiefly our old friends the ex- and dys-academics). Next come part-time bureaucrats such as heads of departments, who are required to combine their administrative responsibilities with academic work. Thirdly, there are the rank and file of university teachers, the level at which the highest concentration of negative-minded mediocrities is likely to be found. And finally, of course, there are the students.

Ideally, each echelon should respect the one above it and trust the one below it. In practice, one often encounters a nutcracker situation, with an alliance between echelons one and three crushing level two between them. When this happens it bodes ill not only for the members of level two, heads of departments, but also for level four, the students.

The trouble is that the only basis for so unholy an alliance is almost invariably detrimental to academic interests. The fearful mediocrities of level three are solely concerned to improve their own position, which they are very likely to regard as threatened by anything which improves the lot of the students. There may of course be universities or colleges where these mediocrities are not the dominant element of that echelon, in which case all is well. But, unfortunately, it is very possible that these negative elements are the preponderating force amongst the rank and file of the teaching staff in your educational institution even if they are in a minority. For the prejudices – under the guise of principles – harboured by such elements are generally very strongly felt and the people concerned are therefore often actively obstructive, whereas most real academics are lovers of peace and do not want to rock the boat. Add to this the top echelon's characteristic cynical disregard for any principle other than politics (in the worst sense of that word) and the equally characteristic jealousy that ex- and dys-academics so often harbour against successful real academics, and you will understand why the alliance between these two elements is so unholy and why the nutcracker effect ensuing upon it is so dangerous to you.

What about an alliance between echelons two and four? This has been known to occur, albeit rarely, but it is unlikely to win against a one-plus-three combination. In a case of which I know, an innovating head of department introduced sweeping changes of which the overwhelming majority of students heartily approved. True to form, a few of the rank-and-file teaching staff opposed these changes and went behind the head's back to the dean, a member of the dominant bureaucratic clique, who lent them a ready ear. The students rallied round the departmental head and most of them signed a petition in his support. But the superior muscle of the bureaucracy

ensured their success and that of their rank-and-file allies,
and before long the department had relapsed into the morass
from which the head of the department, with the active co-
operation of the great majority of the students, had temporar-
ily managed to extricate it. In addition, two staff members
who had protested strongly against the high-handed action of
the bureaucracy were threatened with summary dismissal and
a further two who were loyal to the head found themselves
out of a job soon after when their contracts were not renewed.

Officious officials

There is a growing tendency for universities and colleges to
appoint non-academics to high administrative posts, people
who have never been – and have never had any desire to be
– university teachers. Their background is normally in business or in some other field of endeavour quite remote from
the groves of Academe, such as the armed services. Surprisingly enough, perhaps, they are usually much more successful
as administrators in academic institutions than the ex-
academic bureaucrats who are generally their bosses. Unlike
the average ex- or dys-academic, non-academics have no
hang-ups about teaching, writing or research. They have never
competed in these areas, so they harbour no grudges against
those who are successful in them. As a result, they can
approach their work with an impartiality and objectivity which
so many of their ex-academic colleagues lack. As always, of
course, there are exceptions, notably the sycophants who want
to suck up to their bosses and who are easy to spot with their
phoney posh accents – with the vowels just a little overdone.
But they are in a minority.

I once knew a retired naval captain who was the bursar of
a hall of residence for university students and more senior
academics. He would always have a cheery word for all and
sundry; he would know everyone's name; and he would even
help residents with their luggage if he happened to see them
struggling along a corridor.

In general, he was as helpful as could be and genuinely
concerned for the welfare of his residents. But the friendly
atmosphere was somewhat dampened by the officious attitude
of some of his colleagues, one of whom – an ex-academic,
incidentally – actually made a habit of paying unannounced
visits of inspection to residents' rooms, often in their absence,
and leaving pointed notes threatening condign punishment if

their rooms were not tidied up.

This sort of petty officiousness on the part of someone in authority can easily rub off on his underlings, and the result is quite likely to be a souring of relations between students and staff at all levels. But subordinates are often capable of being unhelpful, officious, authoritarian and rude quite independently of their superiors. We are all familiar with the domineering secretary who insists on protecting her boss from all and sundry and who will interview you at length before even condescending to make an appointment for you to see the great man. In fact, he is often as afraid of her as you are! Another common type is the minor clerk who is quick to dismiss you with a brusque – and usually wrong – answer to an enquiry. I have known students who only discovered too late that they would have stood a good chance of being awarded a valuable scholarship, for which they had been told that they were ineligible. And then there is the petty official who guards even the most trivial piece of routine information as if it were a state secret.

These petty tyrants can take out all their frustrations on students, who are the only class of beings lower in status than themselves. In this regard these secretaries, clerks and minor officials have quite a good deal in common with the equally petty-minded academic mediocrities we have already discussed.

Both groups thrive on gossip and achieve feats of originality and creativity in passing it on that they are denied in any other field of endeavour. Both groups also enjoy nothing better than exchanging stories illustrating the clumsiness, stupidity or general worthlessness of students, as this gives them the ego-boost that they so badly need.

It does not take long to identify a member of this fraternity. Nothing will give them greater pleasure than to see you admit defeat in the face of the brick wall which they have thrown up against you. When confronted with such an obstacle students tend to react in one of two opposite ways. There are those who become meek and subservient before the pocket Hitler, and there are those who become aggressive. Both these reactions are wrong. Kowtowing to a petty tyrant may pay off in the short term, but it is more likely eventually to earn you his scorn than his respect – not to mention the loss of self-respect involved in the self-abasement in the first place. Aggression, on the other hand, will only invite a showdown, in which you will probably be the loser. The answer is to be polite but firm – and then to walk away from the troublesome individual as quickly as possible. Find a way around his brick wall instead of keeping on banging your head against it. This may be easier said than done, but sometimes there is a surprisingly simple solution staring you in the face. The great personage whose secretary has been fobbing you off for weeks may turn out to be quite easily reached by telephone. He may have a direct line which he answers himself, or he may make a habit of working late in his office – with the she-dragon safely out of the way. In that case, you might actually manage to catch him in person. On the whole, for anything at all important a personal meeting is preferable to a telephone conversation and a telephone conversation to a letter. There are exceptions, of course. Where you merely want to inform someone of something and you know in advance that his reaction is likely to be hostile, there is no need to seek him out and precipitate a confrontation. A telephone conversation will serve the purpose far better, and it is also easier to find a brief excuse for ringing off than to turn your back on someone and walk out while he is in full spate. But, if the person you are dealing with cannot be trusted to tell the truth about anything – a surprisingly common problem – and you want to be sure that your position will not be misrepresented, there can be no substitute for a written communication. When dealing with crooks it helps in any case to confirm in writing anything agreed upon verbally.

In general the rule should be to "go to the top". This applies particularly, of course, if the minor official you are dealing with is clearly ill-informed, unhelpful or rude. In such cases it is advisable simply to ask to speak to the person in charge. But it sometimes happens that the person "in charge" is actually less knowledgeable and less obliging than his subordinate. There is that occasional rare gem, the long-suffering lowly official who is always not only irrepressibly cheerful but also delightfully indiscreet and whose every word is to be treasured. His last chance of promotion has long since been forfeited by his irreverence for the organisation where he works, but he knows too much that could seriously compromise his employers for them to contemplate sacking him.

It is, paradoxically enough, the "egalitarian" society in which we live that has undoubtedly produced a great deal of the bitterness and hostility in the work-place generally as well as in the academic work-place specifically. The idea that everyone now has an equal opportunity to rise to the level of his own incompetence has resulted in what has been so aptly dubbed the "rat-race" society. Everyone is thought to be in competition with everyone else, and it is now fairly generally assumed – though hardly ever stated in so many words – that those who find themselves in the lowlier ranks of society must somehow have less "merit" than those who are more "successful" in life. In the much more stratified society of the past, however, it was accepted that a man's position in society had absolutely nothing to do with his "merit" or lack of it but was entirely the result of an accident of birth. It was in this spirit that Lord Melbourne, Queen Victoria's first Prime Minister, could say: "I like the Garter. There's no damn merit in it!" – a gentle hint that, like beauty, merit is in the eye of the beholder. Once one recognised that the fact that a person was a menial worker, servant or clerk did not automatically brand him a "loser", the way was left open to harmonious relations between those at different social levels.

Until quite recently something of this otherwise obsolete ethos survived in Oxford and Cambridge, but even there the "cash nexus" mentality has made serious inroads upon it, so that only a few vestiges of it now remain. When I was a Cambridge don living in college, the college porters, Richard the college postman and Wally the college lavatory cleaner were friends of mine and colleagues in a very real sense. Their love for the college was real and deep, and they felt a sacred bond uniting themselves with the institutions which they served. George Skill, the deputy head porter, for example, enjoyed nothing more than to carve out of polystyrene a representation of the college's ornate sixteenth-century front gate or its breathtakingly beautiful "Bridge of Sighs". Every detail was moulded with loving care, down to every last bar on every last window. I was greatly honoured when he pre-sented me with one of these products of his college loyalty and pride as a parting gift, and I have treasured it ever since.

It saddened me to find that when I happened casually to mention one of these sterling colleagues by name in conver-sation with other dons, they would often not even know who I was talking about. "Doug?" they would repeat quizzically, "Who is Doug?" To me Doug was not just another faceless college porter but a friend with whom I had had many an enjoyable chat. He would come into what was officially known as the "small combination room" – the dons' television lounge – late at night while I was watching the horror film of the week, and, though I did not always appreciate the interruption and he did not always appreciate the film, there would be a little light-hearted banter before he continued on his rounds.

The traditional attitude of a college porter to the students was very much that of the non-commissioned officer towards cadet officers, an attitude which came quite naturally to the many college porters who had a service background. Every student was always punctiliously addressed as "Sir" (a practice which the influx of American students has done something to shake, as they insisted on calling the porters "Sir", the normal title accorded to older men in terms of quaint American usage). But, this token of deference aside, a college porter was always able to exercise a form of authority over the "young gentlemen", and so there grew up a mutual respect, a mutual trust and a form of mutual loyalty between students and "college servants".

By contrast, the Cambridge bedmakers, or "bedders", as they are commonly known, who, by university statute were traditionally required to be "old and ugly", have tended to have more of a modern cash-nexus mentality. When I was a student a new bedmaker once announced herself with the words: "I'm not spick and span, but I like to keep the dirt out." Then there was the bedmaker who had a race with one of her "young gentlemen" every morning to see whether she could finish all the other sets of rooms on her staircase before he got up. Once the other sets were done she would promptly go home and he would be left to make his own bed himself. Another bedmaker would do everything she could to hurry a particular young gentleman out of bed and off to his first lecture because his set of rooms had been selected by the bedmaker and her cronies as the venue for their daily morning tea party.

Those who stick to the letter of the law in order to get away with doing as little work as possible are really only a variant of those officious sticklers for the rules who insist upon ramming every last one of them down your throat. Indeed, there are even some who supplement the official rules with ones of their own devising. One such was the assistant invigilator whom I had the misfortune to encounter during a public examination I was sitting in one of those draughty, cavernous London halls so beloved of examining boards. The candidate sitting at the desk just in front of me had had the temerity to fill in her examination number and other necessary details on her answer-sheets before the official start of the examination. The assistant invigilator, a young woman, descended upon her and threatened her with disqualification if she persisted. The candidate dissolved in tears and the incident is unlikely to have done much to improve her examination performance. In fact, what she had done was not strictly illegal except in the private rule-book of the assistant invigilator, and, even more important, no invigilator had the right to disqualify any candidate for any reason whatsoever, something of which the candidate was not aware at the time of the confrontation.

It is always advisable to check the rules for such things carefully in advance. And don't take some petty clerk's word for it. Get hold of a copy of the official publication in which it is all spelt out. Most educational institutions and examining bodies will be bound to have such a document, and it is quite likely to repay the effort to peruse it at length. This applies not only to disciplinary rules but also to rules for degrees, syllabuses, prerequisites for applying for scholarships and awards, and any other rules your college or university may have. There is of course the old story about the student who claimed a yard of ale in accordance with some obsolete university statute, only to be fined for not wearing his sword when he turned up to collect his prize – an example of one dead letter being used to lay another to rest. But as long as you concentrate on real rules and living laws you should be able to avoid any such embarrassment.

Eminences grises

In a number of universities and other educational institutions around the world there is a committee, board or council of laymen behind the scenes which, though it may leave the day-to-day running of the institution to salaried academics and bureaucrats, has the final say itself and may intervene whenever it sees fit.

Such bodies range from the moribund to the hyperactive and from paragons of honesty and integrity to models of total corruption. The average person goes through his whole student career without any contact with any such organ and often even blissfully ignorant of its existence. But it is just as well to find out exactly what the structure of your educational institution is. The day may come when you will want to appeal over the heads of what you have always taken to be that institution's supreme authorities, in which case you will need to know not only whether there is any such higher authority but also what its composition is in terms of actual names, positions and likely attitudes.

This is easiest when the body concerned is made up of only one person, – usually termed the "visitor" – though even then it is possible to fall into errors of judgment, as the Fellows of Peterhouse, Cambridge, discovered about two hundred years ago. The mastership of the college was vacant and the visitor had the right to appoint his successor. But the visitor's freedom of choice was not unfettered. By dint of custom he was obliged to select the new master from a list presented to him by the Fellows. On this occasion, however, it was known that the visitor, the Bishop of Ely, favoured one candidate and the whole body of Fellows another. What then were the Fellows to do? If they presented the bishop with a list containing both their man's name and his, he would simply choose his candidate, which is what they wanted to avoid at all costs. But the Fellows also could not simply send the bishop a list containing only one name. The visitor had to be given a choice. So the Fellows hit upon a scheme. They asked the Vice-Provost of another college, King's, to allow his name to be used as a "stale", i.e. not a genuine candidate. The Vice-Provost, a man called Barnes, agreed, and the list that was sent to the bishop therefore contained two names, the Fellows' candidate and Barnes. When he saw this the bishop fumed and wrote back saying that as he had the right to choose the master he duly appointed *his* candidate, despite the absence of his name from the list. The Fellows did not let the matter rest. They took the bishop to court and King's Bench found for the Fellows, forcing the bishop to go back to the list and choose the master from there. Needless to say, he chose Barnes – and a lazier, more inept and more hated master the college never had.

Clearly the moral of the story is: know your enemy – something which may be easier said than done if that enemy happens to be the person lurking in the mirror every time you look at it. But the next chapter will help you to handle even that deadliest of enemies.

CHAPTER IV
YOUR WORST ENEMY

Half the things that people do not succeed in are through fear of making the attempt.

— *James Northcote*

Among the very first students I taught at Cambridge (at a time when I was myself still a research student and only a year or two older than my charges) was a quiet, mild-mannered North-country lad whose hands shook like a leaf and whose fingers were stained yellow with nicotine. It was clear that he was highly intelligent, and his work was good – to begin with. Before long he started coming to supervisions without the obligatory essay, and I then received a note from him to apologise for missing the next meeting. I sent for him and he appeared at my door shakier and more bedraggled than ever. He proceeded to pour out a long lament, the burden of which was that Cambridge was not for him and that he felt the only thing he could do was to drop out and return to his home in the North.

He had come from a small grammar school in the North of England, where he had been the all-time star, only to find upon his arrival in Cambridge that he was just another undergraduate: the classic case of the big fish in a little pond becoming a little fish in a big pond. But that was not his only gripe. Cambridge, he whined, was full of aristocrats from the posh public schools, and he was out of place. I pointed out to him that if he wandered through the college courts he would be hard pressed to find more than one or two doors emblazoned with a name prefixed with a "Lord" or "Hon." and that the products of public schools were already in a decided minority throughout the university.

But that is not what he wanted to hear. He actually *wanted* to feel bad about Cambridge so that he could blame all his problems on it. After all, if the cards are stacked against you from the start, how can you be blamed for failing? If he dropped out and returned home, I told him, he would not be able simply to leave his problems behind him in Cambridge. They would follow him wherever he went because they were *within* him. And, though his sense of inadequacy might now be blamed on the university, he would later on blame his job, his wife, his children, his pet poodle – in short, anything or anyone except himself.

One of the commonest things to blame is the past: "My parents were too strict; they wouldn't allow me any independence." There are of course strict parents, but to blame them for everything that goes wrong is really just a cop-out. And don't forget, for everyone who blames all his troubles on an over-strict upbringing there is another who will point the finger at a lack of home discipline: "My parents were over-indulgent; I had too much freedom." What those adopting these two extreme positions have in common is that both of them avoid taking responsibility for their own mistakes and failures. Even worse, by blaming their failures on the past they both regard failure as inevitable, and in so doing actually invite failure.

What happens in practice is that, without realising it, one *teaches* others how to treat one. In my first year as a student at Cambridge, for example, I had a neighbour who had always "just run out" of coffee, sugar, stamps – or even sticking plaster. He never returned anything he "borrowed" (though I didn't mind not getting back the used plaster!) and he kept coming back for more. I had unwittingly *taught* him that I was a soft touch, and the only remedy lay in *unteaching* him. So, when he next came to call, I simply reminded him of what he owed me before he could make another request. After two or three such reminders he stopped using me as a free source of supplies. Did this rebuttal cost me his friendship? Surprisingly, perhaps, it did not. On the contrary, he now viewed me with a new respect and realised that, though I would go out of my way to help a friend who was genuinely in need, I would not be victimised by someone who was simply using me.

Blaming others

Similarly, a false view of reality is presented by such everyday remarks as: "You make me sick"; "her nagging drives me crazy"; "his attitude really makes me cross". Illness, physical as well as mental, *may* indeed be caused by emotional upsets, but no-one can *make* you angry, sick or mad except yourself. It is not what the other person does that causes your suffering but *your* reaction to it. Sigmund Freud was so sure that whatever happened to a person was self-willed that whenever one of his children so much as stubbed a toe he would ask: "Why did you do it?"

Even someone intent on starting a quarrel with you will be

doomed to disappointment if you are determined not to play along, and in my experience there is nothing more enjoyable than remaining cool while the other person is ranting and raving out of control. "It takes two to tango", it has been said, but one might add that it also takes two to *tangle*.

That is not to deny that in extreme cases the actions or words of another may be so provocative as to trigger off an uncontrolled response, but it is worth remembering that even in law provocation is not a complete defence or excuse. A person who is provoked into killing his provoker has to show that any reasonable person would have been similarly provoked, but this does not exculpate him. He will still be found guilty, albeit on the lesser charge of manslaughter rather than of murder.

Once you stop trying to pin the blame for your problems on everyone but yourself, you are ready to tackle the problems themselves and find a solution to them. For example, if you are overweight you are never going to solve your weight problem as long as you blame your condition on your glands, your large bone-structure, your metabolism, the standard of your college cafeteria's cuisine or the stresses and strains of a student's life which force you to overeat. It is only by accepting responsibility for your own eating patterns that you will be able to overcome the problem.

"If only"

This does *not* mean that you must spend your life brooding on your past mistakes and feeling guilty. That sort of behaviour will immobilise you just as much as blaming others for all your own shortcomings, and it will prevent you from getting to grips with reality. One of the most important aspects of reality is recognising that that which is done is done and cannot be undone. Nothing is more debilitating than the little phrase "if only": "If only I had done that"; "if only I hadn't done that"; "if only I hadn't done it that way"; "if only I hadn't lost my temper"; "if only I hadn't told that lie"; or perhaps even, "if only I hadn't told the truth about that".

Analysing past mistakes is one thing, brooding on them quite another. There is no surer way of guaranteeing that you will continue to make the same mistakes than by refusing to learn from the past. At a time when I was working outside the U.K., a student and junior colleague of mine with a happy-go-lucky disposition fell in love with a vintage car which had to be reconstructed pretty well from scratch. The "expert" who undertook to do the work for him kept asking for large sums of money for parts and never had very much to show for it all. Several years and several thousand pounds later the car was still nowhere near completion and my colleague considered himself lucky to recoup a small fraction of what he had paid. He then bought a used car to drive about in, which he subsequently sold to someone who, determined to save himself some money by not paying the local sales tax, kept it in my colleague's name, thus exposing him to liability in the event of an accident. In both cases a less than scrupulous person had taken advantage of my cheerful friend's open and trusting nature. In the second incident my friend could quite easily have made sure the car was transferred into the name of its new owner once it had been sold, but he trusted the buyer to do it for him. He simply had not learnt from his earlier experience, and whenever I broached the subject with him his stock response was: "I don't want to talk about it."

"Next time"

But, if you are going to indulge in post-mortems, how can you avoid the "if only" syndrome? There is a way. Try replacing "if only" with "next time". This will enable you to learn from the past without constant immobilising backward glances and recriminations. "If only I hadn't done that" then becomes "next time I won't do that", preferably followed by a decision as to what you *will* do instead.

But, if you find yourself going over and over your past mistakes in your mind you may easily end up a nervous wreck. After analysing what went wrong and extracting from it some practical lesson for *future* use, you absolutely *must* put it out of your mind. This is not always as easy as it sounds, but it may help to use a sort of formula whereby you banish the subject finally and forever from your thoughts. An effective way is by resorting to paper, preferably a loose piece of paper on which the troublesome topic can be written down and which can then be ceremoniously and eternally consigned to the flames or disposed of in some less dramatic fashion. America's President Eisenhower used to employ a similar technique to dismiss from his mind the names of people he didn't like and with whom he wanted nothing further to do. He would write the name of the offending person on a piece of paper, which he would then bury in a drawer. Unfortu-

nately, it is not always possible for us mere mortals to turn
our enemies into "unpersons" in this way, but I have found
in extreme cases that writing the name of the person on a
piece of toilet paper and flushing it down the loo has worked
wonders. If ever I happened to bump into that person again,
I would find it very hard to dredge up his name from the
remote interstices of my memory to which this little ritual
had banished it!

Living in day-tight compartments?

Sir William Osler, the famous Oxford physician, recommended "living in day-tight compartments", or, in other
words, turning your back on the past. This is presumably
what animals do, living from day to day, but then they probably have no option. For human beings it strikes me as imprac-
tical to insist upon it. People do tend to cast their minds back
to the past from time to time, and, what is more, there is a
great deal to be learnt from it. "The burnt child dreads the
fire" and "Once bitten, twice shy" are two well-known pro-
verbs which underline this simple truth.

Fatalism

But my chief objection to living in "day-tight compartments"
is that it encourages a fatalistic attitude to life, which though
comforting in certain respects can be seriously debilitating.
The ultimate in fatalism is sitting cross-legged in the middle
of London's Kensington High Street on the basis that if you
are destined to be run over by a bus you *will* be run over by
a bus, but if not, not. Even more moderate forms of fatalism
can, however, be a disincentive to initiative. The well-known
case of Helen Keller springs to mind, who refused to accept
that just because she was blind, deaf and dumb she would
never be able to have a normal education, let alone excel in
it. Had she adopted a fatalistic attitude she would probably
never even have attempted to learn to speak, read or write.

Probably the commonest form of fatalism encountered in
the Western world is the tendency to attribute everything to
"luck". The ancients used to divide the calendar into "lucky"
and "unlucky" days, and the current popularity of astrology
and other occult arts panders to a similar outlook. There are
even those who have been persuaded by numerologists to
change their names to more "propitious" ones, as the numerical values of the letters of their old names were "unlucky".
Even people who are not otherwise superstitious are often

reluctant to walk under a ladder and prefer to avoid the number 13 (so that, for example, the Football Pools never have a thirteenth week). Above all, there is the idea at the back of many a mind that some people are somehow intrinsically "lucky" while others are born "unlucky". But it is worth looking behind the "luck" to the other factors at work. As the humorist Stephen Leacock put it: "I am a great believer in luck, and I find the harder I work the more I have of it."

Attributing everything to luck is really just a way of getting off the hook. For, after all, if everything is simply determined by luck, there is no lesson to be learnt from past mistakes (except perhaps that it doesn't pay to walk under ladders or to be one of a party of thirteen around a dinner table).

The best advice is, I think, to steer a middle course, without shutting off the past day by day but also without brooding on it and becoming fixated on it. In that way you will be able to learn from the past while recognising that it *is* past. This position is perhaps most succinctly stated in Reinhold Niebuhr's beautiful prayer:

> "God grant me the serenity
> To accept the things I cannot change;
> The courage to change the things I can;
> And the wisdom to know the difference."

It is perhaps this last gift, the wisdom to know the difference between that which is inevitable and that which is not, which is the most precious of all. Lord Kelvin, the famous scientist and inventor, opined that a heavier-than-air machine would never be able to fly, a statement which he lived to regret. Had the Wright brothers accepted Kelvin's expert opinion, they would have regarded the failure of their experiments as inevitable and would probably not have bothered to persevere. But the opposite danger also exists, of aiming at the impossible. The alchemists' vain pursuit of the "philosopher's stone", which would magically change base metals into gold, is a case in point – though the creation of plutonium out of uranium in a nuclear chain-reaction comes remarkably close to the alchemists' dream!

Provided you don't become fixated on the past, analysing your mistakes can be a powerful learning tool. One of the chief reasons for this is that it is the first step towards taking responsibility for your own actions, and therefore for your own life. This ability is probably *the* single most important

criterion of adulthood, a test which all too many biologically
mature "adults" regularly fail.

Accepting responsibility

It is only by taking responsibility for your life that you are
able to grow mentally and achieve success. It was this sort of
maturity which, for example, enabled Benjamin Disraeli, one
of Britain's greatest Prime Ministers, to overcome his initial
failures. When he finally entered Parliament after four
defeats, his flowery mode of delivery coupled with his eccen-
tric dress (his get-up including a bottle-green frock-coat, a
"network of glittering chains" and a pair of fancy pantaloons)
turned his maiden speech into a fiasco. But he did not resume
his seat before shouting these prophetic words above the
cacophony of hisses, catcalls, howls of derision and hoots of
ridicule:

> "I am not at all surprised at the reception which
> I have received. I have begun several times many
> things, and I have often succeeded at last. Aye,
> sir, and though I sit down now, the time will come
> when you will hear me."

Instead of becoming embittered or despondent, he was able
to learn from this initial setback, and went on to become one
of the finest parliamentary orators and most successful leaders
in English history.

Worry

But responsibility brings with it concern, and, in extreme
cases, stress, worry and anxiety. It is to combat the harmful
effects of these extremes that a motley host of psychiatrists,
psychologists and counselling services of every description
has sprung up all over the western world. Their success rates
vary enormously, but the problem is real enough.

"You do not get stomach ulcers from what you eat," says
Dr Joseph P. Montague, author of the book *Nervous Stomach
Trouble*: "You get ulcers from what is eating you." Medical
science has slowly and reluctantly come to recognise that
purely physical conditions, including heart disease, high blood
pressure, rheumatoid arthritis and even possibly cancer, can
be psychosomatic illnesses, i.e. caused by psychological factors, notably worry and anxiety. This profound truth has only
recently dawned on the medical profession, yet Plato knew
it two and a half millenia ago: "The biggest mistake physicians

make," he pointed out, "is trying to cure the body without attempting to cure the mind; yet the mind and body are one and should not be treated separately."

Recognising worry for the killer that it is is one thing; doing something about it is quite another. Worry often takes the form of a vague, nagging fear which drains you physically as well as mentally. The first thing to do in combating it is to discover exactly what it is you are worried about. Most of the disasters that worriers anticipate every day never happen, the chief reason being that their fears are not based on a realistic assessment of probabilities.

For a student to be in constant terror of examination failure, for example, is senseless. First, in most universities and colleges those who fail their examinations are in a decided minority. But, more important, worrying about failure is actually quite likely to cause it. Worrying is a drain on a person's energy, and a time-consuming one at that. So, the more you worry that you may fail the greater the likelihood that you will!

Having recognised what it is that you are worried about, you are ready for the second prong in your attack on the worry habit, which is to *accept* the worst mentally. If examination failure is your anxiety, imagine that you have already failed and try to picture your reaction to it. Before long you will realise that even something as terrible as failing your examinations will not mean the end of the world.

This will launch you straight into your third prong of attack: planning positively in the event that your worst fears materialise. In the case of examination failure, the first question should probably be: Will I be allowed back to repeat the year? Or, if not, is there anywhere else I can go to finish the course and get the qualification I want? If not, what other options will be open to me and which one should I choose?

This three-pronged attack will not only ensure that, if the worst comes to the worst, you will be ready for it. It will also greatly diminish your anxiety, because the unknown is always much more frightening than the known. And, once you have identified your worry, accepted the worst mentally and planned how to improve upon it, you will have the confidence of knowing that whatever the future holds you will be prepared for it. With your worries banished, you can get on with the job of living.

So, the next step is to think of ways of preventing your fears from becoming realities. If it is examination failure you are afraid of, the answer will be found in Chapter X. But, whatever the object of your anxiety, there will always be some way of preventing it from happening, even if you are afraid it *will* mark the end of the world. A group of people in America, for example, whose chief worry was that a nuclear war would wipe out human life on the planet as a whole, have accepted the worst and improved upon it by moving to a remote part of the country where they have constructed their houses so as to withstand nuclear fall-out and radiation!

Revenge

One of the most gnawing kinds of worry is the spirit of revenge. Avenging yourself on your enemies, especially those of the dirty and devious variety, is a form of rough justice and is often the only justice you are likely to get, as the more devious your foes the less likely you are to have any recourse to law.

Revenge, we are told, is sweet. But think twice before setting out to get even with someone. You are liable to become caught up in an elaborate web of your own making from which it will be very hard to extricate yourself; and your energies will be dissipated in the course of your single-minded pursuit. The Chinese proverb is probably nearer the mark: Before embarking on a course of revenge, remember to dig two graves. Or, as Shakespeare put it:

> "Heat not a furnace for your foe so hot
> That it do singe yourself."

Selfishness

This does not mean that you must "love your enemy", an impossible counsel of perfection which flies in the face of human nature. Like the rest of creation, the human animal is by nature selfish. Sociobiology offers an interesting explanation of this based on examples drawn from a variety of animal species. Among the most apparently altruistic creatures in the world are worker bees, who toil tirelessly day and night to nurture, serve and defend their queen and her offspring, while themselves remaining sterile. The sociobiological explanation is that this apparent altruism is nothing of the kind, as the workers are in fact promoting the interests of the genes which they share with the queen. So, though the bees are not selfish in the ordinary sense of the word, they are the instruments of what has come to be termed "the selfish gene". And a similar explanation is offered for such selfless feats as human mothers rushing into burning buildings in order to save their children from the jaws of an agonising death.

If even such exceptional acts of courage can be accommodated within an overall framework of selfishness, how much easier it would be to explain ordinary everyday human behaviour in such terms. To censure human selfishness from some lofty moral pedestal is therefore as senseless as condemning man for not being able to fly like a bird. Rather, accept human nature for what it is and build upon it.

Many purportedly moral injunctions actually amount to telling you to subordinate your selfishness to someone else's. Religious cults which regiment their followers and subject them to the word of some authority figure provide a good example of this. The individual members are robbed of their freedom, and indeed of their individuality, the resulting state of humility and obedience being held up as amounting to the attainment of the laudable goal of selflessness. This sounds fine until you compare the abject cringing state of the ordinary member with the life of luxury and ease often enjoyed by the leader of such a cult. Selfishness has not been eliminated: the selfishness of the follower has simply been subordinated to that of the leader.

The "we" trap

Part of the problem is the need so many people – and young people in particular – feel of "belonging", of being "accepted" by their peers. It is this need which explains such bizarre happenings as, for example, the mass suicide of the adherents of a religious cult. It also explains such phenomena as drug addiction as well as such comparatively harmless practices as the sudden contagion of a new hairstyle, earrings or a new style of dancing, which is likely to sweep the group-conscious mass of a generation off its feet – at least until a new fad comes along to take its place. The fad of one generation is invariably a comic spectacle to the next. If you have ever seen old films of the Charleston or black-bottom dances of the 1920s you will know what I mean, not to mention the flat-chested pencil-shaped image favoured by the fashionable women of the day.

Beauty, we know, is in the eye of the beholder, and this is never truer than where group indentities are concerned. A particular style of dress, taste in music, mannerism of speech, or a whole new lifestyle, is attractive to the impressionable chiefly because it enables them to join a group and "belong". On the whole there is nothing wrong with this, unless the fashion or practice adopted is one which is criminal, positively dangerous or likely to be injurious to health.

But, identifying yourself with a group of any kind will detract from your individuality to *some* extent. This applies even to the most loose-knit and undemanding of groups, but the closer your identification with the group the greater your subordination to it. Which in practice tends to mean your subordination to some figure of authority. And in this respect the difference between a gang leader and a saintly guru is only one of degree, because both will tend to rob you of that which makes you yourself: your individuality.

The approval of others

Closely related to the need to belong is the need for the approval of others. This is even commoner than the need to belong, as the whole of our educational system and, for that matter, pretty well the whole of our social, political and economic system is based on it! You cannot get a university degree, for example, without the approval of your examiners, nor can you get a job without the approval of your prospective employer – which is unlikely to be forthcoming unless you have the approval (in the form of a confidential letter of reference or confidential telephonic report) of your *previous* employer or of some other influential personage.

Within limits, of course, no orderly society can exist without some degree of conformity on the part of its members. But many people conform much more than is actually necessary. In the hope of furthering their careers they "creep up" to those in authority, sacrificing their own individuality in the process.

Experts

Those whose approval is most often sought are of course the powerful, but hardly less common is the fear of inviting the displeasure of anyone perceived as an expert. There are, for example, those who have lost their lives as a result of taking dangerous drugs prescribed by a medical "expert" who has misdiagnosed the patient's condition in the first place. The average person tends to be afraid of questioning the word of an "expert" – and above all a medical "expert" – by seeking a second opinion. And there is nothing that the mediocre medico hates more than the patient who has the guts to ask some intelligent questions. The true man of science would surely welcome a patient with an enquiring mind, but the mediocrity sees any sign of questioning as a challenge to his omnipotence and often becomes quite testy.

The very terminology employed by the medical profession is calculated to cow all but the most fiercely independent of spirits. Hence the use of such expressions as "doctor's orders", which places the patient firmly under his physician's thumb – not to mention the arcane "medicalese" used at the patient's bedside by one member of the medical fraternity to another. Even the use of the title "doctor" is a clever ploy, as the overwhelming majority of medical practitioners have no doctorates of any kind but only two bachelor's degrees! The title "doctor" arose during the Middle Ages, when ordinary people would address anyone with a university education as "doctor". This was nurtured by the medical profession itself to the point where one now finds one member of the profession addressing another as "doctor" all the time. (It is for the same reason, incidentally, that surgeons, who originally were barbers and did not have a university degree, are to this day stripped of the title "doctor" once they have specialised.)

The medical profession is by no means the only group of "experts" to cow the average citizen into silent acquiescence. Another group with which students are likely to come into contact are psychologists, and educational psychologists in particular. A former student of mine came to History after a brief spell reading for a degree in engineering and a longer but equally unhappy period spent studying accountancy. His first two choices were the result of advice given him by educational psychologists specialising in aptitude testing, though he had known all along that he had no real interest in either engineering or accountancy. But he felt obliged to take the advice of the "experts".

How had these "experts" reached their conclusion? On the basis of a varied battery of tests, in which my student was asked, among other things, such questions as: "What would you rather be, an eagle or a hippopotamus?" But, how can some "expert" get to know you, your personality, preferences, strengths and weaknesses, better than you know yourself – all in the space of a few hours and on the basis of some cryptic questions whose answers have to be heavily interpreted in order to make any sense at all?

*"I'm OK – you're OK"**
But this desire for approval is not confined to situations involving either people in authority or experts. It is even found, for example, in restaurants, where it manifests itself in reluctance to send a leathery piece of steak back to the chef for fear of offending him. And even when the customer does pluck up enough courage to complain, he is likely to be so full of guilt and remorse at doing so that he will fail to notice if his "new" steak is actually just the old piece of boot-leather with the jagged edge trimmed straight (a well-known restaurant trick!).

But is this not at least better than the opposite extreme, the thoroughly obnoxious person who objects to everything on principle and who will send back a perfectly good bottle of wine just to show his girlfriend what a connoisseur he is?

Both extremes should be avoided. The reason for advocating assertiveness (as distinct from aggressiveness on the one hand and undue timidity on the other) is that if you live your life always looking over your shoulder in order to win the approval of others, you are not actually in control of your life at all. Deep down there is bound to be a sense of your own lack of worth, a feeling that you are "not OK", which cannot but detract from your happiness and general well-being.

Happiness
According to the Chinese saying, you need only three things in life in order to achieve happiness. They are:

1. Something to do,
2. Someone to love,
3. And something to look forward to.

In other words, you need to feel needed, a feeling which can easily be distorted to mean a need for external approval. But the two feelings – the need to be needed and the need for approval – are not necessarily the same thing. The sense of need comes essentially from yourself, not from others. "Something to do" should therefore be taken to refer to something that you yourself want to do. "Something to look forward to" likewise sees the future from an internal point of view: some-

---

*Title of a book by Thomas A. Harris, published by Pan.

thing that will give *you* pleasure. And notice that the second criterion is "someone to love" and not "someone who loves you": the motive force once again is outwards from the self and not inwards from other people. In short, as the Romans put it, "Every man is the architect of his own fortune."

But what exactly *is* happiness? Many people seem to expect some great turning-point which will miraculously change their lives for all time. Some who are unhappy in their present situation anticipate a new dawn once the current phase of their lives ends: "When I leave school . . ."; "when I go to university . . ."; "when I start working . . ."; "when I get married . . ."

The environment in which you find yourself should not be underestimated. It can make a world of difference to your outlook on life and to your degree of happiness. But if you pin your hopes on some miracle which will coincide with a change in your external circumstances, you are likely to be disappointed.

It is *your* reaction to your environment which *really* matters – as we saw in the case of my Cambridge student which is related at the beginning of this chapter. What is to be avoided at all costs is *over-reaction* in either direction, which will tend to spoil a stroke of good fortune and make a bad situation even worse. What may appear at the time to be a calamity is unlikely to turn out to be quite as catastrophic as expected, provided you don't react to it in too emotional a fashion. As the Duke of Wellington put it: "Nothing is ever so good or so bad as at first appears."

It is commonly believed that it does you good to get emotions such as anger, frustration or hostility "off your chest". Nothing could be further from the truth. Scientific research has recently discovered that these emotions stimulate the release of the hormones noradrenaline and cortisol. While cortisol is thought to reduce your immunity to infection, noradrenaline constricts your blood vessels and causes your heart to beat faster, which raises your blood pressure. So, far from "clearing the air", in the long term losing your cool could seriously affect your health – and will probably make you feel bad straight away in any case.

Guidelines

How then can you avoid being your own worst enemy? Here are some of the main points of the chapter in a nutshell:

1. Don't blame others for anything that goes wrong in your life. That way you will never be able to solve the problem.

2. Try replacing "if only" with "next time".

3. To banish some unpleasant event from your mind, make a note of it on a piece of paper and then flush it down the loo. The same technique may be applied to unpleasant people.

4. Analysing your mistakes is a powerful learning tool. Don't be a fatalist, but don't become fixated on your past mistakes either.

5. Accept responsibility for your own life, including your mistakes, and go on to overcome them.

6. Worry is a killer, but remember our three-pronged attack on it:
    i   Find out exactly what it is you are worried about.
    ii Accept in your mind the worst thing that could happen.
    iii Plan positively to prevent it from happening.

7. Revenge may be sweet, but remember to dig two graves before setting out to get even with someone.

8. In general there's no harm in joining a group, but beware of identifying with it to the point of losing your individuality.

9. Don't seek the approval of others for everything you do. That way you will never be happy.

10. Remember: *You* are the architect of your own fortune.

11. Beware of over-reacting. The Duke of Wellington's words are worth keeping in mind: "Nothing is ever so good or so bad as at first appears."

12. Keep your cool: "clearing the air" just isn't good for you.

PART TWO

KNOW – HOW

CHAPTER V

HOW TO READ EFFECTIVELY

*Too much reading hinders knowledge. We think we know what
we have read and consider ourselves excused from learning it.*
– J-J Rousseau

Whenever I visit Harvard I make a point of looking up an
old friend of mine who has been a professor there for many
years. Meeting at the Harvard Square T-station, we saunter
across to one of my friend's favourite haunts for lunch and a
lively conversation. One of this eminent academic's pet gripes
is the poor educational background of American students
and, not least, their inability to read profitably. Before lecturing on a new topic, my friend informed me at our last lunch,
he would set his students some introductory reading, but when
he tests them on it, he complained, he invariably finds that
most of them have no knowledge of it.

In the interests of peace and friendship, I refrained from
telling my old friend that I thought it was this method of his
which was at fault and not his much-maligned students. The
students were being thrown in head first at the deep end of
a new area of study without any help or guidance.

"Seek, and you will find" runs the well-known biblical quotation. But the converse is equally true: seek not and you will
not find – because you will not know what to look for and
would not recognise it even if you were to stumble upon it.
To the average student an academic book is likely to be a
formidable obstacle, an undifferentiated mass of words pre-
senting a uniformly baffling aspect. To read it straight through
from beginning to end as if it were a love story or a detective
novel would be a serious mistake. Yet, in the absence of any
specific advice on how to approach academic reading matter
most students *do* tackle it as they would their favourite light
fiction – resulting in the distressing lack of comprehension
lamented by my erudite Harvard friend.

The student of economics, for example, who plunges
blithely into the pages of Keynes's *General Theory* is liable
to find himself in deep waters. This is well known to the

economic fraternity and is the reason for the numerous "keys" to Keynes's thought which have been published.

But what about an apparently straightforward subject like history? The fact that it lacks an elaborate technical vocabulary of its own and that it makes comparatively easy reading may actually be more of a handicap than a help. Sir Lewis Namier's two monumental tomes, *The Structure of Politics at the Accession of George III* and *England in the Age of the American Revolution*, provide an excellent example. They are packed with detail, the significance of which is likely to be lost on the student who does not understand the conceptual framework within which Namier was working.

The comparative approach

Here, as in so many other intellectual pursuits, the comparative approach is invaluable. A comparative glance at the writings of, say, Sir Keith Feiling will at once reveal the established outlook on eighteenth-century English History against which Namier was reacting and will enable the student to read him (and his antagonists) much more profitably.

Ideally, no matter what your subject is, you should use your reading to build up your own conceptual framework, an enjoyable task which will enable you to take a much more constructively critical view of the "authorities" whose writings you are required to study.

It is all too easy simply to coast along passively and take everything you read for granted. And it is alarming to see how many students regularly follow this line of least resistance. The authority of the printed word is awesome. Nor is this tendency confined to students: a good many of their academic mentors are equally incapable of genuine critical analysis, and that even includes some "experts" who have written books on their subject of speciality.

A well-known book on the tyrants of ancient Greece, *Greek Tyrants* by A. Andrewes, is a case in point. Each chapter deals with a different tyrant, and a different explanation is given for the rise of each. It never seems to have occurred to the author that there might be an explanation common to *all* the tyrants which would make sense of the wave of tyrannies that swept through state after state in the Greek world. It also never occurred to him that it might be interesting to examine those states in which tyranny never arose and see whether a common explanation for *that* might be found as well, which would cast yet more light on the states where there *were* tyrannies and on the phenomenon of tyranny. In short, the book lacks the one component that might be regarded as *the* essential ingredient of any academic book: real thought. The reader approaching a book of this kind without a framework of his own is at the mercy of the author and is quite likely to be satisfied, or even impressed, by a work which barely skims the surface.

A word of warning: If your examiner is himself a myopic adulator of some pseudo-intellectual work of stupendous superficiality, take cover. The chances are that he will be even less tolerant than his favourite author. The best bet in such circumstances is to play safe, though that too has its risks, as we saw in Chapter I.

A conceptual framework

But, assuming you are permitted, or indeed encouraged, to adopt a genuinely criticial approach to your reading, how are you to set about constructing a conceptual framework? For that is the only way to ensure that you will get the most out of your reading. A school friend of mine once proudly set out to read the whole of the *Encyclopaedia Britannica* from beginning to end in the mistaken belief that this was the way to increase his general knowledge and turn him into a "master mind". I think he got as far as "LIBI to MARY" before realising that the whole thing was an exercise in futility. Without a conceptual *framework* into which to slot all the newly acquired data they were just so many loose and unrelated jigsaw-puzzle pieces which did not form any picture.

This is of course an extreme case, but reading anything at all without a conceptual framework of reference is likely to prove unproductive.

When embarking upon the study of a new subject area or even of a new topic, don't immerse yourself in one large tome and begin to read it from cover to cover, even if it is *the* prescribed textbook. There may well come a time later on when you will have to do this. But initially you should rather explore the subject and the various approaches to it by sampling a number of different books. In short, adopt a *comparative* approach.

In certain subjects there are some publications available which collect together between the covers of a slim volume a number of divergent views. But even this, helpful though it may be, is only the first step towards the construction of your own personal conceptual framework.

For this purpose the art of skimming is an invaluable tool (see page 88), and the author's preface and introduction, which most students ignore, may just yield a nugget of pure gold. Even the names of the people to whom the author's undying gratitude is expressed for their help and advice may be a clue to his affiliations, something which may otherwise be a dark secret. And the odd autobiographical aside may be more revealing upon reflection than might at first appear. But the chief value of a preface or an introduction is likely to be found in the signposts which it gives to the author's thoughts, the pointers to his motivation and to his place in the spectrum of views on his subject. Occasionally an author will "spill the beans" quite openly in the first words of the preface, giving the reader a revealing glimpse of his purpose in a way which would not otherwise be discernible without reading the whole book closely from cover to cover. A good example of this is to be found in C.B. Macpherson's *Political Theory of Possessive Individualism*, whose preface summarises the whole book in its opening sentence:

> "Some time ago I suggested that English political thought from the seventeenth to the nineteenth centuries had an underlying unity which deserved notice."

Signposting

Many academic books are deficient in signposting. Their authors are often reticent about the direction in which they are travelling, the destination for which they are making and their reasons for choosing one road rather than another, preferring to treat the whole journey as the only one possible and the route selected as necessarily the only right one.

Supplying the missing signposts is one of the most fruitful tasks of the thoughtful reader. But, having filled in the author's signposts you must then put up some of your own. Signposts are essentially concerned with questions: How far is it to the next town? What is the name of that town? What direction must I take to reach it? Is there a choice of routes? Are there any deviations ahead? If I take a wrong turning, where will I land up?

Questions are more important than answers. If you are armed with a question it is generally not too hard to find an answer. Newton was not the first person to see an apple drop off a tree. He was the first to ask why it did so. And, once the question had been posed, the answer was not far behind. But an answer may be staring you in the face and yet be of no use to you if you do not know or understand the problem to which it holds the key. The simple formula $E=mc^2$ encapsulates Einstein's Theory of Relativity and offers a solution to many problems. But, unless you have a problem – i.e. a question – to start with, the formula is of no use to you.

Two stages

There are essentially two stages involved in constructing your own conceptual framework. First you must distil the essence of your reading. This entails building a framework for each of the major works you are using. Only then can you proceed to construct your own personal framework. Let us take these steps one by one.

Five questions

In analysing the writing of *any* author on *any* subject whatsoever there are five basic questions that you must ask. They are fundamental and may appear so obvious that it is easy to overlook them or to imagine that you have considered them when in fact you have done no such thing. It is not enough vaguely to "think about" them. Take a piece of paper and actually write down the five questions and your answers to each. This should be done as briefly as possible without skimping. The same set of questions may be used with reference to a whole book or, for more detailed study, to a single chapter or passage.

We shall use a passage from the Roman historian Tacitus as an example. It deals with the Emperor Augustus (the adoptive son of the murdered Julius Caesar), who, among other things, was accused by some of starting the civil war between the Caesarian party (of which he was the leader) and his adoptive father's assassins: -

> "On the one hand there were those who claimed
> that Augustus had been driven to civil war by filial
> piety and by a political crisis in which there had
> been no room for law – civil war, which could
> neither be prepared nor maintained by honour-
> able means . . . (They also claimed that) there

had been no other remedy for a strife-torn nation than the rule of one man. Nevertheless, the constitution had been organised not as a monarchy nor as a dictatorship but under the title of 'Principate'. The empire had been fenced in by the ocean or by far-off rivers; the legions, provinces and fleets were all linked together; there had been law for Roman citizens and moderation towards the allies; Rome itself had been magnificently refurbished; in the interests of general peace a small amount of violence had been exerted."

(Tacitus, *Annals* 1.9 – my own translation).

What?
The first question to ask of any piece of writing is: *What is the author saying here?* In the passage before us Tacitus claims to be reflecting the views of those who were favourably disposed towards Augustus. The whole passage is therefore made up of purported opinions, which makes it more difficult to analyse than one containing (or purporting to contain) nothing but factual information.

It will at once be apparent that our "What?" question is really an umbrella beneath which lurk several smaller questions, such as: Is Tacitus right in attributing these views to Augustus's supporters? Are the facts upon which their supposed opinions are based true or false? It will help to assemble the bare facts used in the passage first:

1. Augustus started the civil war between the Caesarians and the conspirators who had assassinated Julius Caesar.

2. The system of government under Augustus was one-man rule.

3. Augustus secured the frontiers of the Roman Empire.

4. Augustus instituted an efficient system of administration.

5. Augustus greatly improved the appearance of the city of Rome.

6. Augustus's reign was generally peaceful.

7. Augustus's government employed a certain amount of force.

The last five of these statements are incontrovertible, but numbers one and two are actually opinions masquerading as facts. Whether or not Augustus's reign was "the rule of one man" has been debated from his day to ours, and the question of responsibility for the outbreak of the civil war after Julius Caesar's assassination remains open. So, despite the mention of some genuinely positive features of Augustus's reign in statements (3) to (6), numbers (1) and (2) not only express opinions in the guise of facts but actually adopt an anti-Augustan position! Could this possibly reflect what Augustus's *supporters* were saying immediately after his death, as Tacitus would have us believe?

Our doubts are only heightened when we examine the explanations for Augustus's actions which Tacitus puts into the mouths of the late emperor's supposed adulators. Augustus's motives for starting the civil war are said to be "filial piety" on the one hand and the existence of "a political crisis in which there had been no room for law". Filial piety certainly was an important Roman virtue, but it was also considered wrong to sacrifice public to private interests, and Augustus is here portrayed as starting a civil war simply in order to avenge his adoptive father's murder – a picture more reminiscent of a mobster than of a patriotic leader. As for the second explanation, this too damns Augustus with faint praise. The innocuous-sounding phrase "in which there had been no room for law", under the pretence of justifying Augustus's actions, actually accuses him of being a criminal! And this image is reinforced by the ostensibly matter-of-fact description: "civil war, which could neither be prepared nor maintained by honourable means."

In short, our close analysis of exactly *what* Tacitus says reveals that under the thin disguise of praise for Augustus the cunning historian actually condemns him – something which would be unlikely to emerge from a less methodical reading.

Why?
The second question to ask is: *Why does the author say what he says?* This important question may require a certain amount of detective work to answer, but a close reading of the text itself will often yield valuable clues even without any external evidence. Extrapolating from the biography of the writer and importing such "insights" into his writing can in

any case be an extremely risky undertaking. In literary studies there are even those who believe that the author's intention is irretrievable or, at best, irrelevant to the task of the critic, terming the pursuit after the author's intention "the intentional fallacy". In more prosaic subjects, however, the author's intention is paramount in any reading exercise and without it there is no communication at all.

In the opening chapter of his *Annals* Tacitus makes the famous boast that his history has been written "without hostility or partiality", and his treatment of Augustus in our quoted passage is clearly intended to back up that proud claim. That is why he makes a point of giving – or, as we have just discovered, of *pretending* to give – the arguments in favour of Augustus, followed by a separate chapter containing trenchant criticisms of him and his rule. To the unwary this may well appear balanced and fair, the whole object of the exercise being for Tacitus to emerge with his reputation for impartiality intact while Augustus is damned first by faint praise and then by direct frontal assault.

How?

The next question to ask is: *How does the author say what he says?* This is often of crucial importance, though most students tend to think of it as essentially concerned with "style" and therefore as of no relevance to any subject other than English literature or a modern language in which literary criticism is called for. In fact, like the other four questions, it is relevant to any reading material in any subject of study, though obviously less so in, say, the natural sciences than in the humanities or social sciences.

In the case of our Tacitus passage the style is very down-to-earth and matter-of-fact, which leads us straight into the next question: *Why does the author say what he says in the way that he does?*

Why . . . how?

The answer in this case is quite simple. By employing a deceptively straightforward style Tacitus is trying to persuade us that the views he attributes to Augustus's supporters really were held by them, though we now know from our earlier analysis that this is a false impression.

So what?

The last question is perhaps the most important of all: *So what?* This is a catch-all category designed to bring out the general significance of the passage concerned. Seen from close up an Impressionist painting is likely to look like a series of rough brushstrokes. It is necessary to stand well back from the canvas in order to see it as a whole and to appreciate it as a work of art. So with writing, after peering myopically at it one must take a few steps backwards to see it in perspective. This stage should therefore include some comparative reading in addition to the specific passage or work under consideration.

If one were to compare Tacitus's treatment of Augustus with his handling of other emperors the nature of his prejudice should soon become apparent. Is it Augustus the man at whom the historian's hostility is aimed or is it Augustus the emperor? And, if the latter, is Augustus singled out for attack or is Tacitus generally out of sympathy with monarchy and all its works? And again, if so, why? Comparative reading will show whether Tacitus's attitude towards monarchy was idiosyncratic or whether it was typical of writers of his period and background, and, yet again, if so, why.

Building your own framework

Having analysed your reading in this way you are now ready to construct your own conceptual framework from it. Once again, this will be based on questions, which will vary according to the purpose of your reading. If you are reading in preparation for a particular essay which you have been set, this ought to help you in constructing your framework. Take, for example, an essay in Law asking you to discuss the statement: "English judges are not immune from the charge of political bias on the bench." Here you will presumably read such secondary works as Professor J.A.G. Griffith's *Politics of the Judiciary*, in addition, of course, to a number of actual judgments. But the questions you will ask of these judgments – i.e. the conceptual framework within which you will be working – will be very different from the questions you would ask if your essay were a more normal kind of legal problem. Instead of asking purely legal questions you would now be concerned with the political aspects of the judgments, and instead of a classification in terms of branches of law you would be more interested in classifying them under the name of the judge involved. If, for example, you found that Bloggins J tended to favour employers while Hoggins J gave them short shrift in very similar cases, you might well be on to something. If, however, Bloggins J tended to favour the employer in Employment Law cases but not in Tort, then the chances are that the bias is in the Employment Law statutes rather than in the judge.

But even if your reading is not geared to a specific essay or project, a similar approach should be adopted. Desultory reading is not recommended. It tends to be unfruitful, as we saw in relation to the gripes of my friend the Harvard professor at the beginning of the chapter.

It might be thought that reading with a particular essay topic or problem in mind is blinkered. After all, if you are asked to count the number of *red* objects there are in a room you are unlikely to notice how many *blue* objects there are. Your mind is focused on one particular question and will tend to shut out all extraneous considerations. But what is the alternative? If you concentrate neither on the red objects nor on the blue, the chances are that you will not be aware of the number of either!

What then should you concentrate on when you are reading not for a particular essay or project but just for general study purposes? Dig up a past examination paper, pick a promising question and gear your reading towards it. This will not only give your reading a finely honed cutting edge but will also serve as valuable examination preparation.

Skimming and gutting

When a subject or a topic is quite new to you, such in-depth reading techniques may be a bit premature. What you want at that stage is to be able to go through the material quickly and to pick out its salient features. For this purpose the art of skimming is a must. The way to do it is to take a look at the preface, introduction and table of contents and then to browse through a chapter allowing your eye to travel down the page fairly rapidly lighting on headings and sub-headings en route. The structure of the writing should be used to the fullest. Each paragraph will normally contain a key sentence or phrase and each section or sub-section will generally be intended to convey some main point. If you can identify these the rest of the chapter can safely be skipped. The ultimate test is whether you are able to assemble an intelligible, if rough, summary of the book or chapter concerned.

But, however effective as an introductory technique, skimming is no substitute for real reading, which should always be done with the aid of our fivefold framework of questions.

The one exception is the reading of detailed technical or specialised articles, which are likely to make up the bulk of your reading for essays and dissertations. To wade through the whole of such an article is often unnecessary. What you want to do is *gut* the article, extracting its main point like a pearl from an oyster. Most articles, unlike the majority of books, *do* have a single main point, so the task should not be insuperable. The beginning and end of an article are generally the most important parts. The opening paragraph or two will often point to the findings that are going to be established in the body of the article, and the conclusions are generally summed up at the end.

Speed-reading

One question which I have been asked many times is what the ideal speed is for reading academic material. It is often assumed that though speed-reading may be suitable for light fiction and popular magazine articles, academic material should be ploughed through at a deliberate, dignified, not to say sluggish, pace. Reading speed will of course vary with the degree of difficulty of the material, but most students read far too slowly and can only improve their comprehension by following a few simple rules.

Far from enhancing comprehension, unduly slow reading actually diminishes it. One of the chief reasons for this is that slow reading is often the result of poor reading habits picked up in childhood. Among the commonest of these are vocalisation (i.e. pronouncing the words aloud as you read them) and subvocalisation (saying the words to yourself without actually moving your lips), which slow down the reading process without any compensatory advantage.

Another bad habit is the compulsion to keep going back to the previous line. If this is your "tic" you may fondly believe that it helps you to understand the passage you are reading more clearly, but it actually has exactly the opposite effect. That is not to say that you must never reread a particularly sage remark or an especially difficult concept. Whenever your comprehension of a passage is less than complete you *should* read it again, but when rereading becomes an uncontrollable and senseless urge it must be checked.

Many people follow the words on the printed page by turning their heads from side to side like spectators at Wimbledon's centre court. This and any other kind of physical reading "aid", such as finger-pointing or the use of a ruler to keep your place, actually slows you down by restricting your peripheral vision, with which you would be able to take in much more than just the particular word or phrase upon which your eyes are consciously focused. Another way of increasing your speed and improving your comprehension at the same time is by enlarging your eye-span so that instead of taking in a maximum of only two or three words at a time you are able to absorb as many as five or six. This is done by reducing the number of stops your eye makes to only about two per line, which alone will enable you to double your reading speed from 150 (which is about average) to 300 or more words per minute. The skill involved, however, takes time to perfect and is most effectively learnt on a specific speed-reading course.

As in skimming, so in actual reading it will help you if you can utilise the structure of the material which you are reading. This entails picking out the key concepts as you go along, as discussed under "skimming", above. But reading as fast as your technique and the level of the material will allow is not at all the same thing as skimming. Skimming is designed to give you no more than the *gist* of a book, chapter or passage; fast reading, on the other hand, is intended to yield *full comprehension*. Which is why it is possible to skim a thousand words a minute but the top speed for fast reading is only about half that.

A word of warning: Don't become obsessed with the speed of your reading. Try cutting out inefficient reading habits acquired in childhood, which will increase your pace, but let your criterion always be comprehension rather than speed. And, though it is possible to reach 500 words per minute on light reading matter you will be doing well at 200 words per minute (about 2 minutes a page) on most academic material.

Guidelines

1. Desultory reading is unproductive: read with a specific question or problem in mind.

2. Construct a conceptual framework for yourself, which can be done in two stages:

3. *Stage I*: Analyse all academic reading material under these heads:
    i   What is the author saying?
    ii   Why does he say it?
    iii How does he say it?
    iv   Why does he say it in the way he does?
    v   So what?

4. *Stage II*: Construct your own personal conceptual framework by using the comparative approach.

5. Remember: Questions are more important than answers.

6. Specialised articles should be gutted as a pearl is prised from an oyster.

7. Cut out bad reading habits and increase your speed.

8. But don't sacrifice comprehension for speed.

9. Skimming can be useful – but only as an introductory tool.

CHAPTER VI

HOW TO TAKE EFFECTIVE NOTES

The twelve jurors were all writing very busily on slates. "What are they doing?" Alice whispered to the Gryphon. "They can't have anything to put down yet, before the trial's begun."

"They're putting down their names," the Gryphon whispered in reply, "for fear they should forget them before the end of the trial."

— Lewis Carroll

At a university to which I was once attached students were in the habit of rating their lecturers in terms of whether or not they "gave good notes". This concept was alien to me, and so I was interested to learn that "giving good notes" meant lecturing at dictation speed, preferably with every full-stop and comma called out aloud and every word of more than two syllables written on the blackboard. As this was not my idea of good lecturing, I would begin my course to first-year classes by announcing: "I am not a good lecturer, if that means 'giving good notes'. I do not give good notes. I do not give *any* notes: you *take* notes."

The dictator
Lectures, it has been said, are merely a means of transferring the contents of a textbook from the lecturer's file to the student's notepad without going through the brain of either. The lecture which is read out laboriously at near-dictation speed as if to an assemblage of mindless writing-machines is generally the least valuable kind of lecture. If all it does is to repeat a standard textbook almost word for word there is certainly no point in taking copious notes. What I did when I had the misfortune as an undergraduate to be lectured to in this way is related in Chapter II, which discusses the question of how to deal with the different types of lecturers you are likely to get. Where the lecturer adds no more than a few marginalia to the textbook, then you should do as I did and take the textbook with you into the lecture-room, keep it open in front of you at the appropriate page and, whether the lecturer likes it or not, pencil in the few additions that he makes to the textbook account. These marginal jottings are the only notes

you will need to take in so valueless a lecture course.

To sum up: Just because your lecturer treats you like a dicta-phone doesn't mean you have to behave like one. And the more likely he is to treat you that way, the less valuable his notes are likely to be.

A good lecture does not attempt to replace the textbook but at the same time gives the student the sort of guidance that no textbook – or set of printed notes – can give. Yet, such lectures are generally the hardest to take notes from.

Too many notes?

On the whole, most students take either too many notes or too few. There are those who try desperately to take down every word spoken, with the result that the more fluent the lecturer the less coherent their notes tend to be. I have even come across the odd student who learnt shorthand specifically to overcome this problem. But the game is hardly worth the candle. Shorthand may be quick to write, but it is a laborious and time-consuming process to transcribe, and it takes a good deal of practice before one is able to read back the shorthand directly without transcription.

The chief objection to it, though, is simply that a lecture – a real, live lecture, that is, as distinct from a lifeless reading session – is not intended to be taken down verbatim. If the lecturer knows what he is doing he will be conscious of the difference between the written and the spoken word. The skilful lecturer will therefore repeat his main points for emphasis to make sure that his audience has grasped them. He will embroider them with illustrations to bring them home. And he may throw in a few jokes or light-hearted remarks by way of elucidation. Unlike the mindless robot, the real lecturer will *not* be concerned to stuff your head with facts but rather to kindle the spark of intelligence which he discerns within you.

Whenever I see students scribbling away frantically in an effort to take down a lecturer's every word, I am reminded of the court scene in *Alice in Wonderland*, a quotation from which appears at the head of his chapter. There is also a relevant true story from the Netherlands, where university lectures were given in Latin until well into the nineteenth century. Finding himself blinded by the sunlight streaming into the room, a professor one day casually interrupted his flow to request the students sitting near the windows to draw the curtains. Like the rest of the lecture, this request was couched in Latin: "Claudite cortinas." But, instead of closing the curtains the students simply copied these words dutifully into their notebooks. This marked the end of Latin lectures at that university!

The Dutch students *had* to take down every word spoken, as they had no idea what was being said. They would then presumably have pored over their Latin notes in the hope of making some sense of them. But the same procedure is still used by some students even though *their* lectures are in the vernacular. This is really a waste of time. For one thing, unless the lecturer speaks (or, more likely, reads) at near-dictation speed, it is virtually impossible to take down every word. This means that the notes will be a garbled mess, and no amount of time spent in putting them in order will achieve anything.

But, if you should not take down every word, what approach to note-taking *should* you use? Should you go to the other extreme and take down just a few main headings? In the immortal words of Dennis Jackson's *Exam Secret**: "A skeleton lecture, like a skeleton man, is lifeless. It has very little value." There is nothing wrong with *using* headings in your notes. In fact, any good set of notes *must* have headings, though they can often be put in afterwards. But headings on their own are not enough: they must be fleshed out.

This is usually the point where students are stumped. *What* should you take down and *how* should you make your selection? If the lecture is on, say, the Law of Contract, it would really be a waste of paper and ink to write down even a summary of the facts of a well-known case such as *Carlill* v *Carbolic Smoke Ball*. That information will be found in any textbook on the subject, and lectures are in any case a highly inefficient means of communicating information. What you receive in a lecture is at best second-hand information and generally much more remote than that from the original source.

In addition, the physical circumstances of a lecture are in themselves conducive to error, omission and distortion. For one thing, the average person has only a limited concentration span and the average lecturer is not well versed in the techniques of holding an audience's attention. Secondly, note-

---

*Published as a *Paperfront* – uniform with this book.

taking is always done under pressure, because before you have finished noting what the lecturer has just said he has already moved on to something else – not to mention the mistakes that arise when you try to decipher your scribbled jottings afterwards.

Lecture-notes vs. textbooks

For these reasons it is a serious mistake to try to use lecture-notes as a substitute for a textbook. No matter how expensive – or how bad – a textbook may be, you should always buy at least one per course or section. But, shop around. There is almost invariably more than one textbook available in each area of study. Go to your friendly corner bookshop and browse. The proprietors won't mind unless you look as though you are using their shop as a public reference library. (A bookseller once told me of a "customer" who came in every day to read a particular book, inserting a bookmark to keep his place. One day he finally came up to the counter, book in hand. But instead of buying the book, he simply requested that it be put aside for him as he was going away for a few days and didn't want anyone else to buy it before he had finished reading it!)

Students tend to be intimidated by textbooks, especially by the large doorstop variety, and many textbooks which are religiously purchased are never so much as opened. There are many myths about textbooks which should be dispelled. One is that small textbooks are more helpful than large ones, though others again believe that, however diffuse and unreadable, a large tome is *weightier* than a slim paperback, figuratively as well as literally.

In fact, it is not possible to generalise. There are some truly admirable brief textbooks and some dangerously skimpy ones. Large textbooks, likewise, may be written in the ponderous style that their size seems to suggest, while others are models of clarity and wit. Given the constraints upon time in the examination room, it *is* possible for a candidate to know *too much* and to trip over his extra knowledge as one might on over-long shoe-laces. Such tragic cases may well be caused, at least indirectly, by an attempt to study from a mammoth textbook. But it can be just as disastrous to place reliance upon a small textbook which is so concise as to present an oversimplified picture of the subject or whose explanations are so compressed that they leave you dazed and gasping for air.

Before buying a textbook you should riffle through it, sampling its style and general approach. If the style is so convoluted or the explanations so confusing that you sense at once that you will not be comfortable with it, leave it alone and try another. A good general rule of thumb is often to buy *two* textbooks in each major area of your studies, one big one and one small one. The small one should be selected for clarity and readability and should be used to introduce you to each new section of the subject as well as for examination revision. The big one should be selected for reliability and comprehensiveness and should be used chiefly for reference purposes, in writing essays and generally in supplementing the briefer textbook. It may not be necessary actually to buy the large textbook if your university or college library has good stocks of it, though it is much more convenient to be able to use both books together in the privacy of your boudoir.

So my advice is: Don't bother to take down routine information in lectures, except in brief summary form to serve chiefly as a reminder of what has been covered. For the details you should rely rather on your textbook. You would be wise to concentrate in lectures on taking down material which is not to be found in the standard textbooks. In general, comment, criticism, analysis and opinion are much better suited to note-taking than is factual information. Though, of course, if your lecturer offers you some out-of-the-way information from his own experience or research which has been neglected by the textbooks, then you should most certainly take it down, if for no other reason than that it is likely to crop up in your examination!

The snag is that most students go into a lecture "cold", without any prior knowledge of the topic in hand. As a result the chances are that they don't know when the lecturer is simply regurgitating the textbook and when he is adding some pearl of wisdom of his own. They then come closely to resemble the jurymen in *Alice in Wonderland*, fumbling about and at a loss to know what to take down and what not to take down. Here, as elsewhere, it really pays to have constructed a conceptual framework in the way suggested in the previous chapter.

It is often the throw-away line, the humorous anecdote or the incisive aside – in other words, the things that most students regard as too trivial or parenthetical to put down in their notes – which is the most valuable part of a lecture. One such gem may give you more insight into the subject than a whole sheaf of "regular" notes. And don't imagine you will remember it without bothering to write it down: when you need to dredge it up from the bottom of your subconscious mind you are likely to find that it is out to lunch. So, never mind your fellow-students' scorn of your off-beat approach to note-taking: write down whatever *you* consider valuable and ignore the rest.

No doubt there is the occasional classic remark which is *so* memorable that no one who has ever heard it would be likely to forget it, like the explanation of the difference between desertion and constructive desertion to which a certain law professor of my acquaintance would treat his students: "The husband comes downstairs one morning and says to his wife: 'Darling, I'm leaving.' That's desertion. The husband comes downstairs one morning and says to his wife: 'Darling, you're leaving.' That's constructive desertion." But such unforgettable academic *bons mots* are few and far between, and even one which seems engraved on your memory the moment you have heard it often tends to slip away and get lost in the backwaters of your brain.

Taking notes from books

At one time students used to spend hours at a time hunched over a book in a reading room while laboriously copying out large chunks of it. With the ubiquity of the photocopying machine this practice has largely died out, to be replaced by the amassing of piles of photocopies, most of which are never looked at again. Some students seem to act on the assumption that making a photocopy of a page exempts them from the chore of reading it: its contents will be bound to enter their brains by some form of osmosis. Alas, this rarely happens, though the *judicious* use of the photocopier can certainly save you a great deal of time.

There still are some students, I'm sorry to say, who, while continuing to respect the pristine virginal whiteness of their own books (for fear of losing money upon resale), have no qualms about embellishing library books with their (generally inane and invariably indelible) comments.

The use of the photocopier enables you to mark a book without marking it – i.e. by marking a photocopy of the relevant pages instead. The mesmeric effect induced in so many students by a fluorescent marker is such that they tend to go overboard and highlight practically every line, with the result that the page takes on a characteristic egg-spattered appearance. It is much more effective to mark only the really important words or phrases, and when you want to emphasise a whole passage it is just as eye-catching – and much neater and less expensive – to draw a vertical line with the highlighter in the margin. A less eye-catching but almost equally effective alternative for your own books is a fine vertical line ruled in pencil alongside the edge of the text. For this purpose, as for the fluorescent highlighter, I find the two outer margins preferable (i.e. the left-hand margin for even-numbered pages and the right-hand margin for odd-numbered pages): the marks are more visible there.

Another very useful technique, which can be used on your own books as well as on photocopies, is to write in marginal headings and subheadings. These can be invaluable in finding your way around and may be cross-referenced by means of a private "index" entered on one of the blank pages at the back of the book or sheaf of photocopies. There is nothing more infuriating than stumbling upon some gem in your reading only to be unable to put your finger on it again when you need it. With a private index at the back of each book or compilation you will be able to tell at a glance not only whether the sought-after piece of information is in that particular publication but also its precise page number.

But, valuable though these techniques are, they do not altogether replace the need to take the more traditional kind of notes from books. If, for example, you have just read a chapter or an article which, though relevant, is really not worth rereading *in extenso*, then summarise it or gut it as suggested in the previous chapter. Law students may find it useful to apply a similar technique to cases, arranging the key features of each case under a number of headings: e.g. case-name, reference, date, court, judge(s), facts, decision, *ratio decidendi*, special features. Compiling notes like that is itself part of the learning process as well as serving as a reference tool for revision purposes, and the technique can be adapted to suit almost any subject.

Format
One question which I am constantly asked is: What is the

ideal format for notes? Are notebooks preferable to loose-leaf files or are cards perhaps the answer?

The point is that notes are intensely personal – which is why borrowing someone else's notes is seldom a good idea and why those who send a friend off to a lecture armed with a piece of carbon paper on the assumption that that is as good as attending the lecture themselves are generally disappointed with the result.

The same applies to the physical form which the notes take. If you are a meticulous person generally, the use of a notepad in a ring binder may well be the best solution. You can then interleave notes from your reading between the pages of your lecture notes or add any other additional material when and where you like. The chief advantage of this approach to note-taking is its flexibility, the main disadvantage being that keeping all the loose pieces of paper in order all the time does require a certain amount of fastidiousness.

An even more flexible arrangement without the fussiness is a computer file system, but it has one very serious drawback. Unless you have a computer which is portable enough and silent enough to accompany you wherever you go – including lectures, libraries, laboratories and the like – you will be spending hours and hours keying in all the data from your handwritten notebooks. The value of a computer in writing essays and preparing for examinations, on the other hand, is inestimable, as we shall see in Chapter IX.

Index cards are also extremely flexible, if a bit fiddly. They can be arranged in any order and shuffled as often as you like. New cards can be inserted at any point and rejects removed with great abandon. And best of all perhaps, you can consult a good few cards of your choice at the same time. But cards can go missing with the greatest of ease and, though you may start with all your cards in a humble shoe-box, you will eventually have to invest in some sort of filing cabinet to house them.

If you are less than meticulous and are likely to become bored with the chore of inserting loose sheets into the appropriate ring binders every night or cards into their proper positions, the chances are that you will start allowing your notes to accumulate and before long they will be in a complete and utter mess. So, if you are naturally lazy, rather opt for a less demanding note-taking system. Simply invest in a notebook for the lecture-notes in each of your subjects, with an additional book per subject for notes from your reading. The stoutly bound black variety of notebook is preferable. Inflexible though this system is, it will at least prevent your notes from getting into a state of disarray, and a handsome and expensive notebook should give you an incentive to enter your notes as neatly as possible.

Beethoven always kept a notebook at his bedside so that if he woke up in the middle of the night, his head reverberating with a new symphony, the composition would not have a chance to escape. This may be a little excessive, but you should carry a small pocket notebook on you at least throughout your waking hours for jotting down anything noteworthy when you are not in a formal academic environment. This could be a (probably inadvertently) witty remark made by the Soviet president on television, a pithy advertising slogan, an especially insightful line from the lyrics of a pop song, or a sudden brilliant idea.

This should be done no matter what primary note-taking system you employ. The contents of your pocket notebook can then be transferred to the relevant ring binder, computer file, index card or large notebook at your leisure.

Guidelines

A. Lecture notes

1. Just because your lecturer treats you like a dictaphone doesn't mean you have to behave like one.

2. But don't go to the other extreme either. Remember: "A skeleton lecture, like a skeleton man, is lifeless."

3. Lecture notes are not a substitute for a textbook.

4. Don't bother to take down routine information in lectures, except in summary form to remind you what has been covered.

5. Make a note of the insightful throw-away line, humorous anecdote or incisive aside. It may prove more useful than a sheaf of "regular" notes.

B. Notes in books (preferably your own!)

6. Mark only the really important words or phrases with a highlighter, or draw a vertical line with it in the margin.

7. Write in your own marginal headings and subheadings.

8. Create your own private "index" on a blank page at the back of the book, listing subject and page number.

C. Notes from books

9. Summarise or gut any chapter or article which, though relevant, is not worth rereading from beginning to end.

10. Unless you are naturally industrious, use a hardbound notebook.

11. Otherwise, use a loose-leaf file, index cards or a computer file according to temperament.

12. Remember: Notes are intensely personal. They are there to serve *your* purposes and nobody else's.

CHAPTER VII

HOW TO THINK EFFECTIVELY

*There is no expedient to which man will not resort to
avoid the real labour of thinking.*

— *Sir Joshua Reynolds*

Most people think they can think, but all too often what
passes for thought is in reality merely feeling, sentiment, prejudice or wishful thinking, which is not thinking at all. Everyday speech is full of examples: "I think it's a lovely day"; "he
thinks of her all the time"; "they think the world of you"; "I
think I'll try"; "I really can't think how you manage it!"

Comparison
One cardinal feature which is present in all real thinking is
the element of *comparison*. This is not always apparent to
the naked eye, but there is a tacit comparison involved even
in such simple and straightforward thoughts as: "(I think) this
table is big enough"; "(I think) City is going to win the cup";
or "(I think) there'll be another bus along soon."

How much is "enough"? It will of course vary according
to the question in hand, but it will always involve a comparison
of one kind or another. To decide whether the table is big
enough you have to *compare* its size with that of, say, the
flower-arrangement that you want to put on it. Likewise, to
conclude that City is going to win the cup you will have to
have studied the team's form by *comparison* with its rivals'.
And, unless your remark about the bus is pure wishful thinking, you will have to have *compared* an entry on the timetable
with your watch, or one entry with another (to discover, for
example, that there was a bus, say, every ten minutes).

In fact, whenever you describe something as "big", "small",
"old", "new", "cheap" or "expensive", you are actually
making a tacit comparison. A "big" dog is invariably smaller
than, say, a "big" elephant, but it is not confusing to use the
word just the same, because when we say "Brutus is a big
dog" we automatically compare his size not with that of an
elephant, a hippopotamus or even a mouse, but with other
dogs we have seen. The point is that "big", though it is not

ostensibly a comparative term, is practically meaningless unless we think about it in a comparative way.

In short, you can't think without drawing comparisons, and you can't draw (sensible) comparisons without thinking. Though this simple truth is seldom recognised, it lies at the heart of every academic discipline, despite the efforts of the pedants (see Chapter II) to deny it.

Medicine, for example, essentially entails drawing comparisons between the signs of health and the signs of disease and between the symptoms of one disease and another. So that a patient who presents with a rash of bright red spots will not be treated for measles when he is actually suffering from secondary stage syphilis.

Law likewise has a comparative basis. When, for example, a certain Mrs Donoghue was served a bottle of ginger-beer with a decomposed snail floating in it, she sued the manufacturers for the shock and gastro-enteritis she had suffered as a result of her novel experience. When the case reached the House of Lords two of the judges were for throwing Mrs Donoghue's complaint out, on the ground that even if everything she said was true the manufacturers could not be held liable as there was no contract between her and them (because she hadn't actually bought the ginger-beer herself: she had been "treated" to it by a friend). Lord Atkin, however, in what is now one of the best known judgments in English Law, found for Mrs Donoghue by extending the concept of negligence in the law of tort. Thanks to the support of the other two judges (both Scots, as it happens), Lord Atkin's view prevailed and permanently changed the law. But the point is that both diametrically opposed views applied a comparative approach. The two Chancery judges compared the facts of Mrs Donoghue's case to contract cases while Lord Atkin compared it to cases in tort.

Even the study of History requires a comparative approach, as you can see from a consideration of, say, the causes of the First World War. Few would doubt that the assassination of the Archduke Franz Ferdinand had something to do with the outbreak of the war, but there are probably equally few who would claim that his murder was the sole cause of the war. The point is that there has been no shortage of political assassinations throughout history, but very few have sparked off war. There must therefore have been other causes of the outbreak of the First World War beyond and besides the assassination itself. In short, the question is answered by means of a (tacit) *comparison* between the archduke's assassination and other assassinations. And a similar technique is applied in dealing with *any* question to do with causation, one of the most important aspects of any historical study.

So remember: Thinking involves making comparisons and drawing parallels. Recognition of this fundamental and inescapable fact is surprisingly rare, but it will help you to understand the strengths and weaknesses of the thinking that you come across in your reading and it will also help you in solving problems yourself.

Argument by analogy

All thinking, as we have seen, involves making some kind of comparison, most often tacitly. But the existence of a comparison does not tell us whether the thinking in question is right or wrong. One of the commonest types of dishonest thinking is the argument by false analogy.

Such arguments are often alluring, and the greatest past master of them all in this art of deception was none other than Plato himself. At one point in the famous discussion on justice in Book I of his *Republic*, Plato is anxious to disprove the common cynical view that rulers have their own rather than their subjects' interests at heart. This he does by drawing a parallel between rulers on the one hand and physicians on the other. The snag of course is that it would be easy enough to argue that physicians are more concerned to make money than to benefit their patients. So Plato introduces a little dishonest ploy and maintains that a physician really practises two professions at once: in addition to medicine he practises the profession of a "money-maker". Therefore, in so far as he practises the profession of medicine, he must (by definition) do so in the interests of his patients (as the money-making aspect is now defined as belonging to his "other" profession, that of money-making). Plato is now ready to draw his conclusion: Since physicians practise their profession purely in the interests of their patients, it follows that rulers must practise *their* profession in the interests of their subjects and not of themselves!

This is a typical example of argument by false analogy. Step One in such an argument is to draw a parallel between two things, A and B. In Plato the parallel consists in defining both medicine and rulership as professions – a false analogy. Plato's next step is to introduce a second false analogy – by defining money-making as a second profession on a par with medicine. It is only by means of these two false analogies that Plato is able to reach his desired conclusion, which again is typical of arguments of this kind. Since rulership (A) is similar to medicine (B) in one respect (namely that both are *professions*), it must be similar in all other respects as well. Which means that just as medicine (profession B) is exercised in the interests of the patients, so rulership (profession A) is exercised in the interests of the subjects. Q.E.D.

It is very important to be able to recognise an argument by false analogy whenever you encounter one in your reading. And, believe me, you will, no matter what subject you're studying. But beware. If you try to use the technique yourself the chances are that you won't be able to get away with it as easily as Plato has managed to do – nor for quite so many centuries!

Objective and subjective

Even experts on thinking sometimes fall into serious error. Here, for example, in an extract from a well-known book, Robert Thouless's *Straight and Crooked Thinking*:

> "There must be right opinions even on questions in which the strength of our own emotional inclinations makes it most difficult to find these right opinions. There must be a best way of distributing wealth although it is ten to one whether we are possessors or are not possessors of wealth ourselves will be the strongest influence in determining our opinion of what that best way is." (2nd edition, p. 160).

This passage, I am glad to say, has been rewritten in the most recent edition of the book so as to eliminate the fundamental mistake here. Why, after all, *must* there be a "best way" of distributing wealth? The question to be asked is, surely, "best for whom?" It should then be apparent that what is best for the rich is not necessarily what is best for the poor. It is an unwarranted assumption to take it for granted that there must be a single "best way". The mistake here, then, was to treat as *objective* a matter which is intrinsically *subjective*.

It is of course psychologically satisfying to know the difference between right and wrong, good and evil. Most people would probably be able to agree on a common set of criteria by which to judge a good bicycle, but it would be much harder to achieve unanimity on the criteria by which, say, a painting or a film is to be judged. This is because a bicycle has a clearly determined and universally recognised *purpose*, while a work of art does not. A bicycle is a contraption specifically designed to transport a person from one place to another as safely, expeditiously and economically as possible. The particular make or model of bicycle which achieves all these objectives most successfully will clearly be the *best*. But what is the purpose of a work of art? Is it simply entertainment or amusement? Is it moral edification? Is it purely the perfection of technique? Or is it something more amorphous, the vicarious experience of another mind? Our evaluation of a particular work of art will quite largely depend on the criterion or set of criteria that we choose. And who is to say which criterion is right?

But, if subjectivity runs riot in judging works of art, how much more so will it not do so in the judgment of living human beings, their deeds and motives, their thoughts and attitudes? What I am saying, therefore, is that there is never going to be an objective answer to the question of the "best way" of distributing wealth, and the same applies to most other important social, political and economic questions. It sounds so much more authoritative to say "this is the best solution" than "I think this is the best solution". But beware of this all too common tendency to objectivise the intrinsically subjective.

What is more, unlike the natural sciences, the most important and worthwhile questions in the humanities and social sciences in general tend not to have a right or wrong answer. The reason for this is that the mainstay of scientific proof, the experimental method, usually cannot be effectively used in the humanities or social sciences. If, say, you were to heat up a mixture of chemicals and you got an explosion, it would be easy enough to find out why (provided, that is, that you had an accurate record of all substances and quantities that had gone into the mixture in the first place). All you have to do is repeat the experiment, varying the mixture or the proportions of the chemicals. If, for example, you found that when you omitted the phosphorus no explosion took place, that might indicate that the presence of that element had in some way led, or at least contributed, to the explosion. This hypothesis could then be tested further.

But it would be impossible to discover whether the existence of, say, Napoleon, had changed the course of world history. What would have happened if Napoleon had never been born? We cannot simply "re-run" European history without him as we *could* re-run our chemical experiment without phosphorus.

Argument from authority

The area in which subjective thinking is commonest is that to do with moral values. So, in the longstanding debate on the ethics of abortion, each side rests its case on moral grounds. Those who oppose abortion do so on the ground that abortion is tantamount to murder, while those who advocate abortion on demand deny this and emphasise the mother's freedom of choice. How is one to decide whether abortion is or is not murder? There *is* no universally acceptable objective criterion. The only answer is an appeal to *authority* – that of the Pope or of some religious principle on the one hand, and that of some opposing moral principle on the other. In fact it is probable that most of those on both sides are, without realising it, essentially arguing from authority all the time – if not from emotion, which is even worse.

Syllogisms

The case against abortion could also be put in the form of a syllogism:

> Murder is wrong,
> Abortion is murder,
> Therefore abortion is wrong.

It is important to realise that for an argument to be valid it needs to be judged in terms of two quite distinct and independent criteria. First, is it based on true facts? And secondly, is it logical? As we have already seen, the second premise ("Abortion is murder") is not a fact at all but a highly disputed

point of view. So, even if the logic of the syllogism is impeccable (which in fact it is), this is not enough to persuade us of
its truth.

But, how are we to judge the soundness of an argument's
logic? Here are some simple examples:

> All horses have tails,
> Pegasus is a horse,
> Therefore Pegasus has a tail.

As against:

> All horses have tails,
> Pegasus has a tail,
> Therefore Pegasus is a horse.

And:

> All cats have tails,
> Manxy is a cat,
> Therefore Manxy has a tail.

The first of these syllogisms may not be particularly
enlightening but it passes both tests: both premises (i.e. the
first two statements) are true and the logical form of the
syllogism is sound. The facts in the second syllogism are unim-
peachable, but it fails the second test, as will quickly be apparent from common sense. In terms of the information given
in the two premises, Pegasus need *not* be a horse at all. He
could equally well be a pig, a mouse, an elephant or a giraffe.
The point of course is that though all horses have tails they
are not the *only* animals who are so endowed. So, if we were
to represent all tailed animals by means of a circle, horses
would occupy a smaller circle within it. So far the diagram
would apply equally to syllogisms one and two. Pegasus (in
the form of a dot) should now be placed in the diagram. In
syllogism one his position is clear: inside the *inner* circle (i.e.
the circle of horses). But in syllogism two we can't be sure:
Pegasus could be anywhere inside *or* outside the inner circle.
All we know is that he is somewhere within the *outer* circle
(i.e. the circle of all tailed animals).

As for syllogism three, it has exactly the opposite fault.
Not all cats have tails (for example Manx cats do not have
tails), so though the logic is fine the conclusion doesn't hold
good.

Mistakes like these are surprisingly common, and generally
much less easily detectable than in our examples. The reason
for this is that most thoughts are expressed in ordinary prose.

The moment you restate them in a formal style, as we did
with the argument against abortion, you are in a much better
position to determine their validity. Unfortunately, by no
means all arguments lend themselves to restatement as syllogisms, but you should try it whenever possible. Here is a
syllogistic restatement of a type of argument very often met
with:

> All communists are atheists,
> X is an atheist,
> Therefore X is a communist.

When stated like this it should be easy enough to see that
this is invalid, being in fact a syllogism of exactly the same
type as our second one about Pegasus. The circle representing
"all communists" must be a smaller one within the large circle
of "atheists". The dot representing X must be within that
larger circle, but there is no necessity for it to fall within the
smaller circle of "all communists" as well.

However, when an argument *is* specifically stated in syllogistic form, you should also be on your guard, because the
author may be deliberately drawing your attention to his
impeccable logic in the hope that you won't check the accuracy
of his facts!

Try every possibility
A watchword which I coined as a schoolboy learning Latin
was "Try Every Possibility", or TEP. Latin is supposed to be
a logical language, and so it is (despite the highly illogical
way in which it is generally taught), but even so, a single form
may well have to serve in several different capacities. The
form *portae*, for example, may be either a Genitive or Dative
singular or a Nominative or Vocative plural. All too often a
schoolboy confronted by such a word in a passage for translation will plump for the first possibility until he finds the
right one by means of a process of *differential diagnosis*.

But the usefulness of this technique is not confined to the
learning of Latin. It is applicable to any subject of study and,
for that matter, to life in general. It has often to be translated
to mean *think through every possibility*, a counsel which,
despite its apparent obviousness, is frequently neglected as
the result of the wearing of ideological or other blinkers.

When the Communist Party first took power in Russia in
1917 they decreed equal pay for all. Fyodor Chaliapin, the

famous operatic bass, was duly informed that he would hence-
forth be earning no more than a stagehand. "In that case,"
he replied, "I'll simply *become* a stagehand." Why, after all,
should he spend hours rehearsing and drain his system of
nervous energy on the stage when for the same pay he could
have the carefree existence of a stagehand, a job for which
his massive frame was well suited? This response underlined
a fundamental weakness in the policy of equal pay which had
evidently not occurred to Lenin and his commissars: namely,
that such a policy would kill initiative.

The famous story about Columbus and the egg offers us a
positive example. Challenged to stand a hard-boiled egg end-
up without any external support, the great explorer hesitated
for a moment and then proceeded to tap the egg lightly on
the table, flattening its shell and enabling it to stand! One's
initial instinct might well be to brand this as cheating, but
who said flattening the eggshell was against the rules?

What Columbus did was to think of a novel approach
instead of becoming fixated on the obvious and trying futilely
to balance the egg on its end, as most people do when confronted with the same problem.

Another classic example of this sort of creative thinking is
to be found in King Solomon's judgment in the case of the
disputed baby. Realising that he would not be able to solve
the case by orthodox means, the king hit upon a solution
based on the psychology of motherhood. His offer to cut the
baby in half was a clever ploy, as he knew that the real mother
would prefer to lose her baby to another rather than see it
killed.

Lateral thinking

Today, thanks to the efforts of Edward de Bono, there is a
name for this type of thinking: lateral thinking. As Dr de
Bono has stressed, there is no necessary conflict between
lateral thinking and vertical thinking (i.e. old-fashioned logic).
One should use lateral thinking to find the right approach to
one's problem and then apply vertical thinking to reach a
solution.

In practice, however, there may well be a certain tension
between the two types of thinking. To place emphasis upon
lateral thinking could detract from the less exciting and more
meticulously demanding "vertical" thinking.

A thousand people participated in de Bono's "black cylinder experiment" (as described in his book *Practical Thinking*), in which a tall black cylinder standing on a white table was suddenly seen to fall over without being pushed or touched by anyone or anything visible. The subjects had to explain why this had happened. Well over 20% of them were content merely to *describe* the event, and of those who attempted any kind of explanation most attributed the fall of the cylinder either to some internal mechanism, to magic, to a shift in the centre of gravity, or to the actions of some person or animal concealed from view.

Instead of asking the subjects for a single explanation it might have been more useful to ask each to offer as many different explanations as possible, which would have encouraged them to *try every possibility*. After assembling all possibilities they could then have been asked to reduce them to their essentials, leading to a methodological framework, which would be the most efficient way of reaching the solution, whatever it was.

I remember as a boy listening to a radio programme in which a panel was asked to guess the occupations of the contestants. Some panelists adopted a hit-or-miss approach and would ask a contestant whether, for example, he was a lumberjack. This type of approach was rarely successful. But one panelist would ask instead: "Do you work out of doors?" or "Is it a service?" In other words, he applied *categories*, and his methodical approach quickly narrowed down the area of work concerned. The same applies to any other type of problem. Solutions to the black cylinder problem, for example, could be categorised as follows: the cylinder fell as a result of: (1) some internal force; or (2) some external force. If internal, it was presumably the result of either (a) a build-up of pressure of some kind, or (b) a shift in the centre of gravity, in either case produced by either (i) some internal mechanism, or (ii) some change in the composition of the cylinder. If external, it must have been the result either (a) of a direct blow of some kind, from either (i) a hidden or (ii) an invisible source; or (b) of an indirect force, such as (i) a wind or (ii) a magnetic force. This does not pretend to be exhaustive, but it can be seen that it provides a good framework for detailed testing and an ultimate solution.

Another problem arises from the reluctance to pass judg-

ment on the validity of each proposed solution. Dr de Bono
has coined the word "PO" to represent a sort of neutral position between "yes" and "no". There is perhaps something
to be said for moving away from an unduly rigid and blinkered
"right/wrong" approach to thinking, because, as we have seen,
most major questions do not have a single "right" (i.e. objective) answer. But there is also a danger in giving people the
impression that all answers are equally good.

So, after attempting a lateral solution to the black cylinder
problem, one should be encouraged to follow it up with some
vertical thinking. For example, *could* an internal upward shift
in the cylinder's centre of gravity have the effect of toppling
it over? If not, then that avenue would have to be abandoned
and a valuable lesson will have been learnt for future reference.

Causation
See what you think of this old joke. A man shares a railway
compartment with a stranger in a journey across the Sahara
desert. Every few hours the stranger takes a small tin out of
his pocket and sprinkles some yellow powder from it out of
the window. His travelling companion is intrigued and allows
his curiosity to get the better of him. "I don't wish to appear
rude," he begins rather hesitantly, "but I wonder if you could
tell me what it is you are sprinkling out of the window?" "You
see this yellow powder?" announces the other in a triumphal
tone. "It keeps polar bears away." "But", says the first in an
apologetic voice, "there are no polar bears in the Sahara."
"Precisely!" replies his companion: "It just shows you how
effective it is!"

The joke's humour (such as it is) is based on a logical
mistake technically code-named *post hoc ergo propter hoc*
(literally, "after this therefore on account of this"). I sprinkle
my powder and then find there is an absence of polar bears,
so, since my sprinkling of the powder came first, I wrongly
conclude that it must be the *cause* of the absence of polar
bears. Of course, no one is likely to be misled by our humorous
example, but look out for perfectly serious (and not always
entirely innocent) examples of the same thing!

It is sometimes maintained, for instance, that Britain's
economic decline in the world is the result of the loss of the
Empire, or alternatively, of the introduction of the Welfare

State. Even if it could be proved that Britain's decline did not begin until after either of these events had happened, chronological sequence alone is not enough to establish a causal link.

In fact, the whole question of causation is much more complicated than is generally realised. For a start, what really *is* a cause? There is the true story about the student of History who answered every causal question put to him in an oral examination by saying; "It was the will of God". No amount of prodding on the part of his examiners could elicit from him anything more mundane. They all knew that his answers were not acceptable but at least one of them seemed not at all sure why this was. In his book *Christianity and History* Sir Herbert Butterfield, the famous Cambridge historian, says of the examiners: "We were left completely and permanently baffled" by the candidate's answers. Butterfield is prepared to allow that the candidate's stock reply actually answers the "why?" question but that the question he really wanted answered was the "technical" question: "how?"

This gives the candidate's answer far too much credit and shows an apparent lack of understanding of the true nature of causation. First, if the question was, say, "Why was there a French Revolution in 1789?", that is not quite the same thing as asking *how* the Revolution came to happen. "How?" is a purely factual question and does not ask for an explanation at all. Deep underlying causes would certainly not come into the answer to a "how?" question but would be crucial in the case of a "why?" question.

Secondly, and more importantly, "It was the will of God" is not really an explanation at all but almost a tautology. It is rather like answering the question "Why is it raining?" with the "explanation": "Because there are clouds in the sky."

Thirdly, and perhaps most importantly of all, for our devout examination candidate the will of God is the explanation not only for the French Revolution but for everything that has ever happened. Yet, when we ask *why* a particular event happened, what we are interested in is the factors which *differentiate* that event from other events, not the ones which make it indistinguishable from everything else. So, it is precisely *because* the will of God explains everything that it explains nothing at all!

The term "cause" can be used in two main senses: to refer

to a *necessary* condition or to a *sufficient* condition. A necessary condition is one without which a particular event cannot happen. For example, it is *necessary* that a cause precede the event that it causes, but that is not a *sufficient* explanation, i.e. it is not enough to *make* the event happen. So, if a haemophiliac bleeds to death from an untreated cut, the cut is a necessary condition, because without it the haemophiliac would not have died. But it is *not* a sufficient condition, because hundreds of people receive similar cuts every day without dying. The fact of this particular person's being a haemophiliac is also a necessary condition, but it too is not a sufficient condition, though the combination of the cut with the hereditary disorder does provide us with a condition which is both necessary and sufficient.

Five canons
John Stuart Mill devised five "canons", commonly known as "Mill's Methods", of inductive inference, which provide a useful checklist of causal explanations.

(i)   *Method of agreement*. If, say, ten people who have been guests at the same banquet get food poisoning, the "culprit" will be found by enquiring which food was eaten by them all.

(ii)   *Method of difference*. If in our investigation into the food consumed at the banquet we found that our ten patients had all eaten both the pâté de foie gras and the oysters, we would not know which of the two dishes was tainted and both would be suspect pending further enquiries. We then track down a further eight guests, none of whom took ill but all of whom had some oysters. This proves that the oysters were not at fault.

(iii)   *Joint method of agreement and difference*. By combining (i) and (ii), we learn that the culprit was the pâté.

(iv)   *Method of residues*. If you weigh a container empty, then fill it and weigh it again, the difference between the two weights (i.e. the *residual* weight) will be the weight of the contents. This can be applied in various ways. Our chemical experiment involving phosphorus discussed earlier in this chapter is an example.

(v)   *Method of concomitant variation*. Mill's own formulation of this reads as follows:

"Whatever phenomenon varies in any manner whenever another phenomenon varies in some particular manner, is either a cause or an effect of that phenomenon, or is connected with it through some fact of causation."

(*A System of Logic*, Book III, Chapter VIII, Section 6.)

A good example of this is the observed correlation between cigarette smoking and lung cancer. That, however, is not enough to prove that cigarette smoking *causes* lung cancer, as some defenders of smoking were not slow to point out, but only that there is a causal link of some kind.

Computer thinking

Though computers are capable of processing large masses of data and of solving some very complex problems, the way they "think" is very simple indeed. The binary system on which a computer works recognises only two possibilities at any stage, ON or OFF, translated into 1 or 0, which is reflected in flowcharting.

Imitating this method of thinking is often useful in trying to reduce an apparently complex problem to a simpler form and in that way to understand it better. In fact, our analysis of de Bono's black cylinder experiment employed something roughly approximating to this method.

Here is an ancient brain-teaser to which a similar method can be applied. Protagoras, a contemporary of Socrates, had an impecunious pupil called Euathlus who, unable to pay Protagoras's (pretty steep) fees, arranged with his teacher that he pay him only when he won his first court-case. After "graduating", however, Euathlus did not go into practice as a lawyer and Protagoras sued him for the money he owed.

Protagoras's argument ran something like this: "If I win this case, Euathlus will have to pay me (by virtue of my victory in court). If Euathlus wins, he will have to pay me (according to the terms of our agreement). So, either way, Euathlus has to pay me."

But Euathlus was an apt pupil, and his counter-arguments ran as follows: "If I win this case, I will not have to pay Protagoras (by virtue of my victory in court). If I lose, I will not have to pay Protagoras (according to the terms of our agreement). So, either way, I do not have to pay Protagoras."

Who was right? It will help to analyse the situation in terms of a Yes/No dichotomy:

Will Protagoras win the court-case?
If "Yes":

> (a) Euathlus will have to pay Protagoras in terms of the judgment.
> But:
> (b) Euathlus will lose the court-case.
> Therefore:
> (c) Euathlus will not have to pay Protagoras in terms of the agreement.

If "No":

> (a) Euathlus will not have to pay Protagoras in terms of the judgment.
> But:
> (b) Euathlus will win the court-case.
> (c) Euathlus will have to pay Protagoras in terms of the agreement.

The essence of the problem now emerges quite clearly, namely that each outcome produces not one but two contradictory and mutually exclusive results, one according to the outcome of the court-case itself and the other according to the agreement.

Guidelines

1. You can't think without drawing (tacit) comparisons, and you can't draw (sensible) comparisons without thinking.

2. But beware of the argument by false analogy.

3. Don't be misled into treating as *objective* something which is intrinsically *subjective*.

4. Questions in the humanities tend to be subjective, as no controlled experiments can be carried out to prove or disprove hypotheses conclusively.

5. Look out for the argument from authority – which is generally disguised as something else.

6. Remember the two basic criteria of a valid argument:
   i Is it based on true facts?
   ii Is it logical?

7. If possible, restate arguments in syllogistic form: this will make it easier to test their validity.

8. Remember TEP – Try Every Possibility. Examples: Chaliapin and equal pay; Columbus and the egg; King Solomon and the baby.

9. Think in categories rather than in isolated hit-or-miss fashion.

10. Look out for the "after-this-therefore-on-account-of-this" fallacy.

11. Remember the five canons of causal explanation:
    i Method of agreement.
    ii Method of difference.
    iii Joint method of agreement and difference.
    iv Method of residues.
    v Method of concomitant variation.

12. To simplify complex problems, do as a computer does and think in Yes/No terms.

CHAPTER VIII

HOW TO IMPROVE YOUR MEMORY

Education is what is left when you have forgotten everything that you've been taught.

– Anon

King George III is reputed to have remarked that what distinguishes a lawyer from a layman is not a greater knowledge of the law but a greater knowledge of where to find it. Lawyers typically occupy book-lined rooms and no one expects them to carry every case and every statute in their heads. The only snag is that before a lawyer can repair to his book-lined habitat he has to become qualified – and in order to do so he *will* have to commit to memory large numbers of legal facts. And a similar burden rests on the shoulders of the students of other subjects, despite the fact that in this silicon age of ours there are countless machines which are far more capable of storing and retrieving facts than even the most efficient human memory.

The mud principle

A young nephew of mine recently entered an international Bible quiz. The questions were of a factual nature, often requiring a detailed, not to say minute, knowledge of trivia. I offered to fire some questions at him by way of rehearsal, and among others I asked him to name the Assyrian king mentioned in the Book of Isaiah. Instead of Sennacherib, the name I was looking for, he ventured Darius, a *Persian* king who lived nearly two centuries later.

The problem was that my nephew had been preparing for the quiz on what I call the "mud principle". If you fling mud at something or someone, some of it is bound to stick, and the more mud you fling the more of it will stick. Applied to the memorisation of factual information this entails reading the relevant material over and over again in the hope that it will somehow lodge in your brain.

Framework

As with reading (see Chapter V), so with memorisation, it is necessary to have a *framework* of reference. This my nephew clearly did not have. Constructing a framework of reference for the purpose of memorising factual information is very similar to building a conceptual framework as explained in Chapter V, so not much need be said about it here.

In my nephew's case it would have been necessary for him to go outside the Bible itself in order to build the requisite framework. He ought at least to have familiarised himself with the history, customs and religious beliefs of the different peoples impinging on Biblical history to develop some chronological and geographical points of reference. Just reading the Bible itself and trying to steep yourself in its details directly is rather like trying to learn Russian by plunging straight into the original text of Tolstoy's *War and Peace* without any prior knowledge of the language.

Practically every schoolboy is told at some stage of his career who painted the Mona Lisa, yet only a small percentage of them seem to remember this fact. Why? Is it because they have naturally retentive memories and the rest do not? Probably not, because those who don't remember that particular fact are quite likely to remember something else – whether it be the annual rainfall of Chile, the atomic weight of manganese or how many centuries W.G. Grace scored – which those who remember the fact about the Mona Lisa do not.

The key here is *interest*. If you have an intrinsic interest in a subject, you *will* remember a lot of facts about it which anyone lacking your interest will regard as a bore. There is even the strange case of the railway clerk who knew the whole train timetable off by heart while he was on duty in his little kiosk but who was quite unable to recall any part of it once he knocked off work every evening. This again represents a form of interest. The clerk's interest in the railway timetable was confined to office hours only, during which time this knowledge was a great asset to him and one on which he rightly prided himself. But once his day's work was done he had no further use for or interest in the timetable and could push it into an inaccessible corner of his brain until the following morning.

So, if you really want to master a subject, develop a genuine interest in it. This may be easier said than done, but it is worth realising that every subject is fascinating to someone, no matter how boring it may be to everyone else.

Closely related to this is the desirability of having some

purpose in mastering the subject. The keen philatelist, for example, is likely to know every variation in the colour, perforation, water-mark, paper and cancellation of a large number of stamps, and particularly of those he is actively looking out for. Similarly, the serious punter is likely to know a good deal about the form of a number of race-horses, and not least the horse on which he has just placed a substantial bet.

As far as academic subjects are concerned, what this means is that, strange as it may seem, you will learn facts much more easily if you do not set out merely to learn facts. You would probably have much more trouble remembering, say, the details of Louis XIV's wars if you were just to sit down and learn them for their own sake than if you were grappling with an essay asking you to assess how successful Louis XIV's foreign policy was. In the latter case, you would have a *reason* for remembering the facts and this would provide you with a ready-made *framework*.

If you want to illuminate a minute spot in the dark, there are two ways of doing it. You may light a match and hold it directly over the spot itself. You will now be able to peer myopically at the spot and get quite a good view of it. But another way of doing it is by throwing a floodlight right around the whole field in which your minute spot happens to be. This will not only illuminate the spot but the whole area around it as well. Above all, you will no longer see the spot in isolation but *in context* and *in perspective*. This is what a framework can do for you. By placing the trivial details that you have to learn *in context* and *in perspective* it enables you to *understand* those details and therefore to *remember* them.

Association

In fact, a framework is really just a special case of what has long been known to be the chief key to memory improvement: association. Two-and-a-half thousand years ago the Ancient Greek poet Simonides advised his pupils to go and stand in a different place for each new fact that they wanted to remember, the idea being that they would associate the fact with the place and would therefore remember it more easily. As a schoolboy I found, quite by chance, that when revising material which I had read while travelling on the bus, I would see in my mind's eye the scenery of the places the bus had been passing at the time. This helped to fix the material in my memory. And I have also found it easier to recall the details of a conversation by picturing the scene where it took place.

Another use for this type of association is in remembering names. For a number of years I used to lecture to a class of over 350 university students several times a week. I had photographs of all of them, which I kept before me in alphabetical order, and I would pick on individual students by name to answer questions. In this way I found I soon learnt most of their names, my memory being greatly aided by the fact that each student normally stuck to the seat which he had occupied in the first lecture. This gave me a mental "group picture" of them, and I would notice at once if anyone was "out of place" or if any new face suddenly intruded into the picture.

This "geographical" type of association may not work for everyone and is hard to learn. A much easier form of association to use is one based on the similarities between words. If you are good at punning, this should come quite naturally to you. In fact, many people use it all the time without being consciously aware of it. Which is why learning a language closely related to your own is always easier than learning one totally unconnected with it. Here, for example, are the opening words of the Lord's Prayer in the earliest of the modern artificial languages, Volapük:

> "O Fat obas, kel binol in süls, paisaludomöz nem
> ola! Kömomöd monargän ola! Jenomöz vil olik, äs
> in sül, i su tal!"

Even if you knew that this was the Lord's Prayer, it would be very hard to recognise the words, most of which appear quite alien. Not surprisingly, the heyday of Volapük was short-lived (and, in any case, the surfeit of umlauts made it unsuitable for the typewriter!).

In reaction against the awkwardness and difficulty of Volapük, some breakaway Volapükists devised what they called *Idiom Neutral*, in which the same passage becomes much more readily intelligible, especially to anyone familiar with Latin or any of the Romance languages:

> "Nostr patr kel es in sieli! Ke votr nom es
> sanktifiked; ke votr regnia veni; ke votr volu es
> fasied, kuale in siel, tale et su ter."

Language learning

One of the most useful and enjoyable applications of this sort of verbal association *should* be to the learning of languages – and practically all the languages of Europe are related to one another. Yet the use of derivatives in language teaching is strangely undeveloped. I remember once bumping into a professor of Classics who informed me that he was attending beginners' classes in Italian in preparation for his forthcoming long leave in Florence. "But don't you find that you already know a good deal of Italian from your knowledge of Latin?" I asked. "Not at all," came the reply: "They are, after all, two quite different languages."

The crassness of this answer is of course typical of the pedantic mentality (see Chapter II), which is unfortunately so prevalent today. But, in utilising the relationships between languages, there are certain pitfalls to avoid. When I first taught beginners' Latin to a class of university students, I wrote the Latin word *iacet* on the blackboard and asked for an English derivative from it. Quick as a flash came the reply, from a student who was beaming from ear to ear; "jacket". Now, anyone who knows the first thing about Latin will realise at once that an English word containing the letter "k" is extremely unlikely to have a Latin origin. Every language has its own distinctive pattern of sounds, and you will have to learn some of the unwritten rules by which the words of one language are converted to those of another. So, for example, the Latin word *bonus* ("good") becomes *bon* in French, *buono* in Italian, *bueno* in Spanish, *bom* in Portuguese and *bun* in Rumanian, each showing its own characteristic sound-pattern. But these are no isolated examples. The same patterns keep recurring throughout each language. So, for example, the "o" in *bonus* is not alone in going to "ue" in Spanish. It is a change which regularly affects an accented "o", as in *nuevo* ("new", from the Latin *novus*), *puerta* ("door", from the Latin *porta*) and *muerto* ("dead", from the Latin *mortuus*) to mention but three of the commonest examples.

Books on memory sometimes suggest that in learning a language you should build up your vocabulary by associating words in the foreign tongue with English words which just happen to *sound* like them. To remember that the Spanish word *hermano* means "brother" you should therefore think of the name "Herman" and imagine that you have a brother of that name! This technique is highly inadvisable unless the language you are learning is totally unrelated to English (e.g. Chinese or Basque), otherwise it can actually endanger your ability to use the genuine historical links which exist between languages. The Spanish word *hermano*, for example, *does* have some English relatives: not the name "Herman" but the words "germane" (meaning "relevant" or "closely related") and "german" (as in "brother german", meaning a full brother as distinct from a half-brother or the like). It will not take long to realise how close these English words are not only to the sound of the Spanish *hermano* but also to its sense. If you knew one or both of the English words already, they would help you to remember the Spanish word. And if you had never come across either "german" or "germane" before, you would be killing two birds with one stone, improving your English vocabulary at the same time as your Spanish!

Mnemonics

You may have seen motor cars emblazoned with the emblem of a fish and wondered why this symbol is so closely associated with Christianity. It is, in fact, one of the oldest mnemonics in the world. The initial letters of the phrase (in Greek) "Jesus Christ, Son of God, Saviour" spell the word *ichthus*, which is Greek for "fish" and which also happens to be particularly suitable because of the fishermen amongst Jesus's disciples.

Mnemonics are a very valuable study aid and inventing them can be great fun. If, let's say, you wanted to remember the names of "the Five", the famous group of nineteenth-century Russian nationalist composers – Balakirev, Mussorgsky, Borodin, Rimsky-Korsakov and Cui – a good way would be to form a word or words from the initial letters of their names. As all of them start with a consonant we can use any vowels we like to fill them out. We might perhaps come up with BoMB RoCk, where the capitalised letters represent the composers' names. (The "k", which in any case is silent, may be excused on the ground that it will serve to remind us of Rimsky-Korsakov's double barrel). But, how can "BoMB RoCk" remind us of these Russian composers? We might perhaps imagine them all assembled together in their tailcoats condemning rock 'n roll music: "Bomb Rock!" With this vivid scene firmly fixed in our mind's eye, we should have no trouble remembering the five names. It is surprising what a head start an initial letter gives you.

The same technique can be applied to the memorisation of

much more complex material as well. Let us say you've prepared an essay on the political prejudices of English judges,
in the hope of finding a question on it in the examination.
There are seven main divisions to your essay and it would be
absolutely fatal for you to forget any one of them. So you
form a mnemonic out of the initial letters of each of the
subheadings, which are taken from chapter headings in J.A.G.
Griffith's *Politics of the Judiciary*: *I*ndustrial relations, *P*ersonal rights, *P*roperty rights, *M*inisterial discretion, *C*onspiracy, *S*tudents, trade *U*nions. As the order doesn't matter,
with a slight shuffling of the capitalised letters this gives us
PIP SCUM or, perhaps better, SCUM PIP, which we could
easily imagine as an opprobrious label hurled by the judges
at their detractors: "Oh, you are nothing but a lot of *scum
pips!*" In the examination room you should jot your mnemonic
keywords down vertically rather than horizontally, to give
you plenty of room to fill in what each letter stands for. A
mnemonic of this sort could be further elaborated by having
sub-mnemonics tacked on to each letter to represent, for
example, the relevant court-cases in each category.

The shopping-list approach

In the examples we have considered, the order of the items
to be memorised did not matter. If you need to remember
things in a particular order only occasionally, then you can
use the ordinary mnemonic technique and simply put numbers
against each of the keywords after filling them all in. You
will find that once you have got all the keywords in front of
you your confidence will grow tremendously and their proper
sequence will readily come to mind. In fact, it is a good idea
to number all your keywords anyway – according to the sequence in which you want to handle them – even if the order
is not crucial, because in numbering them you will be planning
and organising your examination answer. Your mnemonic
should then look something like this:

6.   *S*tudents
5.   *C*onspiracy
7.   *U*nions, trade
4.   *M*inisterial discretion
2.   *P*ersonal rights
1.   *I*ndustrial relations
3.   *P*roperty rights

As each category is dealt with, you should tick it off and then turn your attention to the next number.

Most memory-improvement books spend a lot of time on techniques for use in memorising a shopping list in a fixed order, though heaven only knows why a shopping list's order should be so crucial (unless you expect to run out of money before you're able to buy everything you need!). As these techniques are time-consuming to learn and inflexible to use, they are best ignored unless you are really going to use them a great deal. All the different systems boil down to the same thing. You first have to learn a fixed list of keywords, the first representing the number one, the second the number two, and so on. Then you have to link the first item on your list to this number one keyword, the second item on your list to the number two keyword, and so on. One of the commonest is the TEA, NOAH, MAY sequence, with T(ea) standing for one (because a capital T has only one vertical line), N(oah) for two (as the printed n has two vertical strokes) and m(ay) for three (the m having three vertical lines). Let's assume that the three things on your shopping list are, say, shoes, belt and teddy bear, in that order. You now have to picture the shoes floating in a huge cup of tea; Noah wearing the belt prominently over his flowing white robe; and teddy dancing merrily round a maypole. You may of course prefer to use your own keywords, but once you have adopted or devised a set of numerical keywords you have to stick to it.

Memory and thought

If your course largely entails rote memorisation you can be quite sure it is not of a very high intellectual level. As every computer well knows, facts on their own are merely *raw data*. When processed they become *information*, but you can't make a silk purse out of a sow's ear, or, in computer jargon, GIGO, "garbage in, garbage out". The final stage, which is beyond the capability of any computer, is to turn information into thought.

Guidelines

1. Don't rely on the "mud principle".

2. Construct your own framework of reference.

3. It helps to develop an *interest* in what you are studying.

4. Having a *purpose* aids the memory.

5. Even purely factual information is more easily learnt in a problem-oriented framework.

6. Remember: You may illuminate a spot in isolation by lighting a match over it and peering down myopically – *or* you may throw a floodlight all around it and see it in perspective.

7. *Associate* what you want to remember with places if you can.

8. Verbal associations are even more useful, not only in language-learning but in any subject.

9. But if you *are* learning a language, use the natural links that exist with English rather than artifical ones – unless the language you're learning is totally unrelated to English, e.g. Turkish, Basque or Chinese.

10. Devise your own mnemonics: they should be fun.

11. Don't bother to learn special techniques for "shopping-list" memorisation unless you *have* to remember lots of things in a fixed order.

12. Facts are raw data. Remember the sequence: raw data – information – thought.

CHAPTER IX

HOW TO WRITE EFFECTIVELY

Take care of the sense, and the sounds will take care of themselves.

– Lewis Carroll

An author and a neuro-surgeon met at a cocktail party. "I'm very pleased to meet you," said the surgeon: "When I retire I plan to become an author too." "Oh, what a coincidence!" replied the author: "When I retire I plan to become a neuro-surgeon."

The point of course is that, though no one expects to be able to perform brain surgery without years of training, most people think that there is no particular skill involved in writing. "I could have written a book about it" is a common enough expression. No wonder that when Edward Gibbon respectfully presented a volume of his monumental *Decline and Fall of the Roman Empire* to the Duke of Gloucester, all that royal worthy had to say was: "Another damned, thick, square book! Always scribble, scribble, scribble! Eh! Mr Gibbon?"

At one time most tests and examinations were oral. Hence, for example, the name "tripos", which is still used for the examinations of the University of Cambridge. The word is the same as "tripod", a three-legged stool, because that is what you sat on to answer questions fired at you in your oral examination. The written examination was taken over from China, where it had long been used as the means of selection for the civil service. But even after the introduction of written examinations in England, tutorial essays and other written assignments were not always taken as seriously as one might expect. In certain Oxford colleges essays on the topics most frequently set were available for a consideration from the porter's lodge, and the less academically inclined did not even try to hide the provenance of their essays. A rowing blue who had hired an essay on Greek tragedy, when reading the essay aloud to his tutor kept referring to "the poet Bophocles".

127

Exasperated by this display of ignorance, the tutor eventually interjected: "Don't you mean Sophocles?" To which the oarsman replied: "But it says here 'Bophocles', sir."

Tackling the essay topic

Now that written work is so ubiquitous and essays, reports, term-papers and the like often count as much as a full-blown examination, it is vital to know how to approach them. Yet, despite its importance, it is only very rarely that students are actually taught this technique.

"WHEN ALL ELSE FAILS, READ THE QUESTION". This old wag's remark contains a piece of sage advice coupled with a shrewd comment on human psychology. It is surprising to see how many students there are who misread the question. In an examination this may be more understandable (if no less inexcusable), not only because of pressure of time but also because it is always tempting – though generally fatally so – to "convert" a title you can't handle to one that you have prepared! But, there is absolutely no reason to misread the title of an essay which you are permitted to write at your leisure and in the privacy of your boudoir. But, don't wait for all else to fail before reading the title: do it straight away.

But *reading* the title isn't enough. You also have to analyse it. You must ask yourself:

    i   What *kind* of question is this?
    ii What are the sub-questions lurking beneath the surface?
    iii How am I to approach them?

These three questions must be constantly in your mind while you are doing your preliminary reading. As we saw in Chapter V, desultory reading is useless. You must construct a conceptual framework before plunging into detailed reading, and the three steps just listed are the way to achieve this. Let's take them one by one:

(i) What kind of question?

The two basic categories are *descriptive* and *discussion-type* questions. You may think it will be pretty obvious to which of these categories a question belongs, but that is not always the case. "Was Nazism specifically German?" (from an actual Cambridge Tripos Part II paper) looks like a perfectly straightforward factual question, but a little reflection will reveal that it is nothing of the kind. There were, after all, plenty of other fascist parties in Europe at the same time as Nazism and you would have to analyse them to see whether there were any elements which Nazism shared with them, whether in terms of success, popularity, methods, organisation, origins or ideology (if any). You might also be able to find resemblances to Nazism in certain non-fascist regimes, such as that of the Soviet Union.

Above all, it would be important to analyse the basis of Nazism itself in terms of traditional German patterns of thought and feeling. So, despite the deceptively simple wording, the question may be rephrased to read: "'Nazism was specifically German.' Discuss."

The operative word in most discussion-type questions is "discuss", but "comment" and "consider" are also found and mean very much the same, and "evaluate" likewise demands a similar critical approach. In poorly worded questions set by examiners who have *not* actually adopted a discussion-type approach in their teaching, the word "discuss" can sometimes be so ambiguous as to leave you in doubt whether what is wanted is a genuine discussion or a mere description. E.g. "Discuss Napoleon's domestic policy." In a properly set genuine discussion-type question, the issue to be discussed should be indicated. E.g. "Discuss the *degree of success* of Napoleon's domestic policy." But, when in doubt it is advisable to treat the question as a discussion-type question wherever possible, even if the word "discuss" (or any other similar operative word) is missing. E.g. "Write an essay on Napoleon's domestic policy."

What exactly is the meaning of "discuss"? Coming from a Latin root meaning "to shake out in different directions", a discussion should *air* the question thoroughly, give the reader all the different points of view – or at least the main ones – on the question in hand and indicate the strengths and weaknesses of each. But that doesn't mean that you must sit on the fence till the iron enters your soul. It is usually advisable to come out clearly and decisively on one side or the other, though most good discussion questions don't have a single "right answer" and you *shouldn't* be penalised if your conclusion doesn't happen to agree with the one your examiner or marker favours. Of course, that does not mean that you *won't* be penalised if you disagree with him, as we saw in Chapter I.

The best questions are open-ended, by which is meant that they do not restrict you in any way, e.g. "'Constitutions should be short and obscure.' (Napoleon I). Discuss." You are of course free to agree or disagree with the statement, but, more than that, you would be quite entitled to say that the length and style of a constitution are irrelevant considerations – provided you argued your case and didn't just make bald assertions. Nor would you be precluded from looking at the statement from Napoleon's point of view and asking what he meant by saying constitutions *should be* short and obscure. Was he perhaps viewing the question from the vantage-point of the ruler rather than the subject? And, if the constitution *were* obscure, how would that affect the rôle of the courts, and how would *that* in turn affect the rights of the citizen?

Where the topic is phrased as an actual direct question there tends to be less leeway. So, if your question read, "Why was the 'revolutionary tradition' so powerful in nineteenth-century France?", it is at least arguable that you would not be entitled to maintain that the "revolutionary tradition" was *not* really powerful at all. If you went on to show why the "revolutionary tradition" *appears* to have been so powerful even though it was not, a tolerant examiner might be able to restrain himself from blue-pencilling your whole effort as irrelevant, but it would probably not be worth taking a chance in the case of a pedant. In any event, it is clear from the wording that you are *meant* to accept that the "revolutionary tradition" *was* powerful, and you would therefore be placing yourself at a disadvantage by arguing against this.

Gobbets

What many students dread most of all is the "gobbet" question, short passages for comment. Here the operative word is generally just "comment" and it is up to you to decide what is worthy of comment in the passage before you. In other words, *you* have to set your own questions – which is why this kind of exercise is such a bugbear to so many.

You should begin by analysing the gobbet in terms of the five questions discussed in Chapter V: What? Why? How? Why . . . how? So what? But, this scheme is for the benefit of your own understanding and appreciation of the passage, not a plan of your answer. And beware of merely writing a précis of the passage. That is not what is required. Elucidating difficulties in the text is of course a different matter altogether. So that, if, for example, the author appears to be praising something when in fact he is being ironical, you should certainly say so.

There is often one particular point to a gobbet, and this is especially the case with very short gobbets. But identifying it will seldom be enough. You must unearth the fundamental question lurking within it and then proceed very much as you would in dealing with a discussion-type essay.

Legal problems

The legal problem, a peculiarity of Law courses, is essentially a variant of the discussion question, though within very narrow confines. Here you are given the facts (or some of them) of an imaginary case and are asked to "advise" one or more of the parties concerned. This entails identifying every possible relevant legal claim that could emanate from the facts you have been given. Your answer will be largely based on previously decided cases. As no one actual case is likely to be identical to yours and as there often are conflicting precedents, you will have to weigh up the different possibilities one against another – which will be the nearest approach in this type of question to a genuine discussion.

(ii) The sub-questions

Having decided what kind of question you have before you, whether in an essay title or in an examination paper, you are ready to move on to the next step: What are the sub-questions? It may not always be apparent that there *are* any, but it is a very rare question which does not have a cluster of sub-questions lurking beneath it.

Take, for example, a question reading: "If anyone was to blame for the outbreak of the First World War, it was Austria." Discuss. This is an open-ended question, and so you will have to consider all possible "culprits" as well as the possibility that no one country was "to blame" or the idea that the whole concept of "blame" is out of place in a serious historical analysis of cause and effect.

For the purpose of your own preliminary analysis it does not much matter where you begin, but the idea is to allow one question to lead on to another until you are left with an unanswerable question. So here, you might start with our old friend, the Austrian Archduke Franz Ferdinand, whose assassination sparked off the outbreak of war. To accept that his death was *the* cause of the war and leave it at that would be superficial in the extreme, but the assassination could certainly serve as a useful starting point. Since we are concerned with "blame" we should ask whose fault the Archduke's assassination was, which in turn will lead us into the whole question of the relations between Austria and the Serbs, opening out into the relations between Austria and the Slavs in general, including the Russians. *If* Austria was to blame for the war, which is the proposition we have to test, we must obviously look also at her relations with Germany. We shall then have to change our tack and consider Germany, Russia, France, Britain and the Serbs as possible "culprits".

As you can see, this far from exhaustive analysis has already yielded a fistful of sub-questions, each of which must be answered, in the process of which sub-sub-questions will be seen to sprout. As we have already discovered (see Chapter VII), questions are more important than answers, and our sheaf of questions will provide us with an excellent basis for our essay-plan.

(iii) Approach

We are now ready for step number three: How to approach our clutch of questions, sub-questions and sub-sub-questions. There is no single right answer to this any more than there is to the main question posed in the essay title itself. The best thing to do is to write all your sub-questions down on one side of paper, either one under the other or in bubbles all over the page. The order does not matter. You then have to work out, on a separate sheet of paper, a possible plan of action, listing all the sub-questions and sub-sub-questions in the order in which you want to deal with them. If one plan doesn't work, scrap it and start again on a fresh sheet of paper. Do this as many times as necessary until you are really satisfied. The chief criterion should be a *logical* order and a natural *flow* from one section to the next. You want to avoid non-sequiturs and any jarring effect. Above all, ask yourself whether a total outsider who knows nothing about the subject would be able to follow your argument and find your conclusion irrefutable. If so, you are probably on the right track.

Planning and reading
After this analysis, make a provisional plan for your essay. This will be more concerned with questions than with answers, as you ought not to have done your detailed reading yet, only some preliminary browsing and skimming, in the way shown in Chapter V. The steps taken so far will point your reading in the right direction, so that you can now immerse yourself in the most daunting of tomes without fear and, above all, without getting lost. Instead of reading aimlessly as most students do, you will be reading with a purpose, keeping your battery of questions, sub-questions and sub-sub-questions in mind all the time. This will enable you to save a great deal of time, as you will use the table of contents and index of each book to guide you to the specific sections that you need.

Argument
Most students seem to work on the assumption that when writing an essay you should do all your reading first and only then start writing. This is a highly inadvisable approach to adopt, and one which is wasteful of effort. However questioningly you may read, it is only once you actively start grappling with the question in hand – *in writing* – that you are able to get the most out of your reading. *So, my advice is to start writing your essay straight after going through the four steps just enumerated.*

Above all, this will force you to think the whole thing through and develop your lines of argument. There are essentially two types of logical argument, inductive and deductive, both of which have been dealt with in Chapter VII. By deductive logic is meant arguing from the general to the particular, while induction moves in the opposite direction. Syllogisms are therefore a form of deductive logic, whereas arguing by analogy and all causal explanations are forms of induction. In general (despite the drubbing that induction has received at the hands of certain philosophers, notably Hume and Bertrand Russell), what is known as the "scientific method" rests heavily on inductive logic. Science ideally takes nothing for granted, though there are in practice in every discipline a number of *axioms* which form the bedrock of the subject but cannot themselves be proved.

Newton's experience with the apple is a good example of

induction, as is the story about James Watt and the kettle. In Newton's case the observation and analysis of an apparently trivial event led eventually to the construction of a general theory, and in Watt's to a practical application which was to revolutionise transportation.

If deductive logic is less noticeable than induction in intellectual arguments, this is probably because it tends to be assumed rather than expressed. But it is no less important. In law, for example, most cases are ultimately based on a deductive argument of the type:

> Neligence is a tort,
> The defendant was negligent,
> Therefore the defendant is a tortfeasor.

This may seem too obvious to need expressing. Yet there are cases where it would certainly have helped if the thinking involved had been more clearly recognised. One such concerned a certain Mr Wheat who was spending the summer as a guest at the "Golfer's Arms" in Yarmouth when he fell to his death down the pub's back staircase. The late Mr Wheat's estate sued the brewery company which owned the pub, with some interesting results.

In order to establish negligence it is necessary to answer three questions in the affirmative: (i) Did the pub owe Mr Wheat a "duty of care"? (ii) Was there a breach of this duty? And (iii) Did this breach cause Mr Wheat's death? The judge found that the brewery company was *not* liable, and the case then went to the Court of Appeal and ultimately to the House of Lords, with the same outcome each time but with three very different patterns of answers to the relevant questions, as you can see from this table:

	Judge	Court of Appeal	House of Lords
Duty of care?	Yes	No	Yes
Breach of duty?	Yes	No	No
Cause of death?	No	No	No

The wide discrepancies revealed here indicate, at the very least, a lack of agreement on the criteria to be used – an area where further deductive reasoning could prove most helpful.

Conclusion

Though, as we have seen, genuine discussion-type essays demand that you weigh up all sides of the question, this should not stop you from coming out on one side or another. The ability to think a problem through to a conclusion is an important asset and should be recognised as such by your examiner or essay-marker. Unless, that is, the arguments you have used to reach your conclusion are so illogical as to be reprehensible or unless your examiner is so prejudiced that he will not accept any answer other than the one that he considers "right" (see Chapter I). Ideally, of course, the conclusion you reach should be less important than the means by which you reach it. But tolerance is all too often respected more in the breach than in the observance.

"Thus we see"

The "thus we see" syndrome is particularly to be guarded against. If the question is anything to do with, say, Frederick the Great, the examiner is treated to a long and discursive biography of that monarch, heedless of the actual question set, and then to a concluding paragraph reading: "Thus we see that Frederick the Great was indeed a devious schemer" (or whatever the question said).

Irrelevance is one of the commonest of student faults and is rightly heavily penalised. Analysing your title carefully and planning your essay as I have suggested will save you from this serious pitfall. It can be quite effective actually to *start* your essay with your conclusion, along the lines of the old debating advice: "First, tell 'em what you're gonna say; then say it; then, tell 'em what you've said." This will indeed ensure that your essay sticks to the question from beginning to end, especially if each of your subsequent paragraphs is essentially a "because" backing up your pre-announced conclusion. Giving your conclusion in the very opening paragraph will also save you from long (and generally irrelevant) introductions and will show the examiner that you have actually thought the whole thing through *before* putting pen to paper!

So, remember: it is not enough to read the question: answer it too – the question actually set and no other. You will get no credit, but indeed quite the reverse, for parading "extra" information which you may happen to know but which is irrelevant to the topic in hand, though *relevant* additional points can help you very considerably.

Style and content

The Lewis Carroll quotation at the head of this chapter is of course a clever variation on the old adage: "Take care of the *pence* and the *pounds* will take care of themselves." As recast by the Duchess in *Alice in Wonderland* it is excellent advice on writing, harking back to the Latin saying: *Rem tene, verba sequentur* ("Hold fast to your subject and the words will follow").

What all this boils down to is: Concentrate on *what* you're saying rather than on *how* you are saying it. This is (if you'll excuse the pun) sound advice. If you really understand your subject your language will be clear, which generally means simple. Obscure and involved language often betrays woolly or non-existent thinking, and affected writing is not only a sign of arrogance but generally also results in sacrificing sense for effect.

To test your degree of clarity in communicating your thoughts you should always read over what you have written. Preferably leave it for a few days so that by the time you come to read it you are no longer so familiar with it as you were while immersed in it. This may help to give you something of that outsider's eye that is so valuable an attribute in self-criticism. Imagine you are reading words written by someone else and look out particularly for any mistakes, contradiction, repetition, gaps, ambiguity or unclearness of any kind. This advice applies to tutorial essays but, for reasons of time, *not* to examination answers.

Format

To subhead or not to subhead, that is a question which plagues many a student. The inane rule given to generations of schoolboys that in an essay you do not have any subheadings is often carried over into tertiary education. In fact, of course, the judicious use of subheadings can greatly aid the author's thinking as well as the reader's comprehension. So, unless it is absolutely *verboten*, or at least frowned upon, in your particular institution or subject, I would strongly recommend you to try it.

Another thing to watch is your paragraphing. Students tend to go to one of two extremes here. They either start a new paragraph for each new sentence or else allow their writing to run on for pages without a break. Both are equally bad. A paragraph should express a single composite idea, with one sentence being the "theme" sentence, and no paragraph should ever be longer than half a page of average handwriting.

Punctuation and spelling

As we saw in Chapter I, little things like spelling and punctuation can be of surprising importance, especially if your examiner has what I call the petty-language-fixation. But even if he is not so afflicted, these small points can be crucial to your results – punctuation because it can make all the difference in the world to the sense, and spelling because it can quickly create a fatally bad impression in the examiner's mind.

The rôle of the humble comma is often underestimated or ignored. Compare these two sentences:

"Laws which restrain the rights of the individual should be abolished."

And:

"Laws, which restrain the rights of the individual, should be abolished."

In the first sentence the implication is that there are some laws which restrain the rights of the individual and others which do not. It is the abolition of the restraining laws *only* which is advocated here. The second statement lumps all laws together, the implication being that all laws *by definition* restrain the rights of the individual and *all laws* should therefore be abolished. And yet, the only external difference between the two statements is a couple of commas!

Like punctuation, spelling is best learnt by observation. "Hard" words and technical terms should receive special attention. There is really no excuse (other than consistency, perhaps) for the student who, after spending a fortnight in the library hunched over large tomes on the Peloponnesian War, produces a ten-page essay in which the word "Pelopennesian" occurs no fewer than forty-five times. (This is an actual case: what surprised me most of all was that he should have got a vowel wrong rather than the number of p's, n's or s's, which are much commoner errors!) And if you are ever in doubt about the spelling of a word, look it up. I am familiar with the typist's lament, "How can I look it up if I don't know how to spell it?" – a veritable Catch-22 situation – but trial and error works wonders.

But, as we saw in Chapter I, even the most trivial of errors can prove fatal to you if you happen to land a petty-minded perfectionist as your marker or examiner. So, take care! Though, as we also saw, the reverse phenomenon is also found: the examiner who goes overboard on an affected style and will give the best mark to the writer of the most dazzling prose, no matter how mindless it may be. But, do your homework first and find out exactly *who* is going to mark your work and what his predilections are before risking something like that!

Word-processing

Of course, if you are writing your essay on a computer or word-processor, you can easily get a program which will check your spelling for you, though this is not much good unless you learn from it, because it is unlikely that your word-processor will be permitted to accompany you into the exam room.

Word-processing can also be used to solve a much more serious problem, what is commonly called writer's block: the fear of committing yourself to paper. The seeming finality of writing does terrify people, including some professional authors, and all sorts of solutions have been devised to get over it. One well-known author does all his writing in an attic which can only be reached by means of a ladder propped up against the window. Every morning the author climbs the ladder and, once safely inside his sanctum, kicks away his single contact with the outside world. Unable to escape, he is forced to work until a prearranged time, when the ladder once again makes its appearance at the window.

A former student of mine found a less radical solution to the same problem by writing everything – including all examination answers and the final draft of his Ph.D. thesis – in pencil. The knowledge that he could always rub it out evidently freed him from the fear of committing himself irrevocably. If you are tempted to try this approach, first check what your university or college thinks about pencil examination scripts, and remember that pencil does tend to be more illegible than ink and considerably fainter.

For essays written at home word-processing is certainly the

answer. You can add, delete and edit to your heart's content, so you need never feel that "this is it", though some writers have found that it *is* possible to rewrite too often, with the result that the best draft has been consigned to oblivion and replaced by an inferior afterthought. If you save everything you write to disk (as you should), you will automatically have copies of all your essays on file in case anything should happen to your "hard copy". Word-processing also gives you much greater flexibility in regard to your essay plan than any other method. You can easily reconstruct the whole architecture of your masterpiece with just a few format commands – and just as easily go back to your original structure.

Guidelines

1. Writing, like neuro-surgery, requires training.

2. Remember: When all else fails, read the question. But it helps to do so *before* waiting for everything else to fail!

3. Also, reading the question isn't enough: you must *analyse* it.

4. Ask yourself:
   i   What *kind* of question is this?
   ii   What are the sub-questions lurking beneath the surface?
   iii How am I to approach them?

5. An answer to a discussion question should give the reader all the main points of view.

6. But that doesn't mean that you must sit on the fence till the iron enters your soul. On the whole, it is best to come out decisively on one side or the other.

7. Remember, there is no "right answer" to a genuine discussion question. But see Chapter I on examiners' prejudices.

8. *Gobbets* needn't be such bugbears if you keep these points in mind:
   i   You essentially have to set yourself your own questions.

    ii   Analyse the gobbet in terms of the five questions discussed in Chapter V.

    iii   There is often a single point to a gobbet, but identifying it isn't enough. You must go on to discuss it.

9.   *Legal problems* entail identifying all possible relevant legal claims.

10.   In tracking down sub-questions don't let up until you're left with an unanswerable question.

11.   Write down all your sub-questions and sub-sub-questions in random order and arrange them in a logical and flowing construction.

12.   Next, make a provisional plan for your essay.

13.   Now start doing your detailed reading.

14.   Remember: It's silly to do all your reading first and only then start writing. Rather adopt this sequence:

    i   Analyse the question.

    ii   Find the sub-questions.

    iii   Devise a logical and orderly approach.

    iv   Make a provisional plan.

    v   Do your detailed reading, having done a good deal of browsing and skimming throughout steps (i)–(iv).

    vi   Research each sub-question and write as you go along.

15.   Pay close attention to the logic of your arguments. Remember the functions of both inductive and deductive logic. See Chapter VII for more on thinking.

16.   Come to a definite conclusion but don't fall prey to the "Thus we see" syndrome.

17.   Avoid irrelevance at all costs.

18.   Remember the old debating advice: "First, tell 'em what you're gonna say; then say it; then, tell 'em what you've said."

19.   Don't worry about your style, as long as your writing is clear: "Take care of the sense, and the sounds will take care of themselves."

20. Watch your format:
    i   Use subheadings unless they are *verboten*.
    ii Start a new paragraph for each new composite idea.

21. Spelling and punctuation can be crucial.

22. Remember: Petty-minded examiners have petty hang-ups, including linguistic perfectionism, otherwise known as the petty-language-fixation. So beware! (See Chapter I for details.)

23. Use a word-processor if you can: it will certainly help to overcome "writer's block".

CHAPTER X

FACING THE FIRING SQUAD

Examinations are formidable even to the best prepared:
for the greatest fool may ask more than the wisest man
can answer.

– Charles Colton

Reading, memorising and learning

"But I read my notes through 37 times!" I have heard this kind of tearful lament from a distraught examination candidate on more than one occasion. The assumption dies hard that all you have to do is go through a regular ritual of reiterated reading and that by some magical osmotic process you will absorb the relevant knowledge. The sad truth is that no matter how good your notes may be no amount of reading will be enough to learn them. *Reading and learning are two different processes.*

And confusing learning with rote memorisation is equally fatal. Even if your examination is of a purely factual nature (in which case you should realise, and make your examiner realise, that it is not of university standard!), you will actually find it easier to learn the facts concerned by placing them in a conceptual framework, as we saw in Chapter VIII. *Parrot-fashion swotting is fine for parrots. If you are not a parrot, it's not for you.*

The blind men and the elephant

Once upon a time there were five blind men who just happened to come upon an elephant. Never having encountered an elephant before they decided to investigate. One explored the elephant's massive flank and announced gleefully to his companions: "You know, an elephant is exactly like a wall." "Not at all," said the blind man who was holding the elephant's tail: "An elephant is just like a rope." "No, no, you are both wrong," retorted the third blind man, who had got hold of the elephant's ear: "An elephant is like a huge leaf." "A leaf?" countered the fourth blind man, who had bumped into the elephant's leg: "No, I'd say an elephant was more like a great tree-trunk." Meanwhile the fifth blind man, who had grasped the elephant's trunk, was equally convinced that an elephant was a kind of snake.

This old allegory points up the need to fit details into a framework if they are to make sense, as we saw in Chapter V (on reading) and VIII (on remembering). The importance of this advice cannot be stressed too much in preparing for an examination.

The syllabus

The first thing to do in preparing for an examination is to familiarise yourself thoroughly with the syllabus. This should be done at the very beginning of the year. There may be a printed syllabus, but don't take it on trust. Syllabuses are interpreted by lecturers and examiners – and not always in the same way.

My father, when a schoolboy taking his *Abitur* (final school examination) at a German "Gymnasium", had a rather nasty experience. His Classics master, affectionately known as "Willie der Waldaffe" (Willy the Ape), had told his charges to "bracket" (i.e. omit) some of the lines of Homer prescribed by the official syllabus. When the government inspector came to examine him, my father was asked to translate just such a "bracketed" passage. He was about to remark on the fact when "the Ape" gave him a deadly look, and he was obliged to translate the passage sight unseen, which, fortunately for him, he was able to do.

That of course was an oral examination. There is less risk of something like that happening in a written examination, and, if it did, all the candidates would at least be in the same boat. But that does not diminsh the need to study the syllabus and analyse it carefully. It is vital, above all, to discover the *scope* of the course, the *approach* and the *depth* in which it is to be studied, information which is less likely to emerge from a printed syllabus than from your lectures and tutorials and from past examination papers.

A crucial piece of information to elicit as early as possible is: Do you really have to study the whole syllabus or are there parts of it which can safely be omitted? This may depend on the format of the examination paper or on informal practice. It may be, for example, that there has always in the past been a choice of four questions out of, say, a total of ten and that one particularly troublesome section has cropped up only twice in the last five years, and then only in the shape of a single (different) question each time. From this information it would seem hardly worth the effort to spend any time at all on the offending section. And it is often better to skip a section altogether than to prepare it in a half-hearted fashion, which might just give you the false confidence to attempt a question on it, generally with disastrous results. But do make sure the format hasn't been changed in the meantime. Finding a new compulsory section made up of topics which you haven't even touched upon is the kind of surprise that you can manage to live without!

But don't restrict yourself to four sections which are *bound* to yield one question apiece. Even if they do, they may not all be to your liking. So give yourself some leeway.

Another important question is the degree of centrality of the section or sections that you choose to leave out. In, say, a Mercantile Law paper it may be quite safe to omit the section on international trade but it would be folly to leave out the sale of goods section, even if comparatively few questions were set on it. The principles of the sales of goods are the basis for foreign as much as for domestic sales, but the special features of international trade do not carry over into the home market.

You will not be able to make your selection without some exploratory reading and an overall picture of the subject as a whole – in other words, without at least a tentative conceptual framework, which should be constructed as suggested in Chapter V.

Learning from your essays
In the course of the year you will undoubtedly be kept busy writing essays and the like, but don't think that this is enough to prepare you for the examination with the addition of a last-minute spurt.

Your essays should be treated as a springboard and not as a prime goal in themselves. Get hold of past examination papers at the beginning of the year and compare any essay title you are given with all other questions set on the same section over the past four or five years. If, for example, you have an essay to write on some aspect of Napoleon III's domestic policy and you find a past examination question asking for a comparison between Napoleon III's religious policy and that of Napoleon I, you will realise that it is useless studying one Bonaparte without the other. The particular question in the earlier paper is unlikely to recur, but some other comparison may be asked for. This is worth bearing in mind in working on your essay, and once the essay has been safely handed in you should return to the library to prepare for a much broader range of topics, using your essay as a nucleus.

Use the reading, note-taking, thinking, memorising and writing techniques suggested in the previous chapters to prepare answers to past examination questions and to questions of your own devising. It is a good idea to ask your lecturer or tutor if he would be so kind as to look over these and "mark" them. Such external criticism can be of inestimable value, and knowing that your private work is going to be "marked" should spur you on all the more.

As the examination draws ever nigher you should prepare short essay plans encapsulating the whole content and lines of argument of each question on a single side of paper. You should cover your whole syllabus in this fashion, and it is from these brief "capsule answers" that you should work out the mnemonics (see Chapter VIII) which you will use to recall them in the examination room.

Test yourself frequently – in writing. It is all too easy to persuade yourself that you "really know" something if you have half an eye on your notes while supposedly testing yourself. There is no one easier to cheat than yourself. Also, it is not enough to remember your mnemonics. If that is all you know you may not be able to answer the questions because you will not remember what the mnemonics stand for. The mnemonics are essentially deep-frozen answers to potential examination questions, so it is vital to see in advance whether you will be able to thaw them out and serve them up to the examiner's palate.

If your "capsule answers" cover the whole syllabus – i.e. the whole of your own personal syllabus – thoroughly and are carefully prepared, there should be no need of any frantic outside reading in the three or four weeks before the examination. But this will depend on your subject. Some subjects do not lend themselves to the "capsule" approach as readily as others and additional material *will* have to be assimilated.

This should be done according to the guidelines suggested in Chapters VI and VIII.

Time-management

Most books on study methods strongly advise students to make a timetable and stick to it. This is easier said than done and many students don't like feeling that they are tied up in a straitjacket, albeit one of their own making. The chief benefit of a timetable is to ensure that each subject or paper gets its fair share of attention, but provided this is so there really is no need of a rigid timetable. And it may be found that some subjects actually need more time to master than others. This will be a personal matter for you to work out. It will depend very largely on the degree of difficulty of the subject on the one hand and on your own knowledge, interests and aptitudes on the other.

What is more important than sticking to a fixed timetable is making sure that you get the most value out of each day. That doesn't mean you've got to feel guilty if you spend any time enjoying yourself or just goofing off. But it does mean that you should *manage* your time actively and not just allow it to slip through your fingers like the grains of sand in an old-fashioned hour-glass.

When you want something done, it has been said, ask a busy man – because a busy man is usually a good time-manager. A useful experiment to test your time-management skills is to keep a detailed diary for just one day, noting down everything you do as the day wears on. Don't trust yourself to remember it all at the end of the day. Carry the diary on you all day and as each hour strikes enter what you have done for the past sixty minutes. It can be painful to realise how much time you waste, but it can also be a salutary lesson.

The most important thing in planning your time is to *prioritise*. Many people spend their days busily on trivial things while major undertakings remain undone. So, plan each day in advance, but not necessarily to the extent of pinpointing the hour and minute when everything is to happen. Your plan should be in writing, preferably in a pocket diary. Top-priority calls on your time – including your academic work among other things – should be marked with an asterisk. Then, when actually living that day, always select the prioritised commitments in preference to less important activities. Tick off each item as you do it, so that your diary serves as a record of accomplishments as well as plans, and the discrepancy between the plan and the reality can be seen at a glance.

For how many hours a day should one study? This is a question I have been asked by scores of students, and my answer is always the same: How long is a piece of string? Once again, such questions will depend on individual capabilities and needs. What one person can master in half an hour may take another a month. In general, however, it will be found that most students are able to work for much longer stretches at a time, if they really want to, than they would otherwise have thought possible. It is also generally true that as the examination approaches you can cover far more ground than you could earlier on. The reason for this is largely will-power and determination, probably *the* most important factors in achieving *any* goal (see Chapter IV).

Another frequently asked question is: for how long a stretch should one study a particular subject or topic? On the whole, the more complex or advanced the subject the longer you need to get your teeth into it. To stop after some artificially prearranged limit, say an hour, would then defeat the whole object of the exercise. The best advice is to go on until you reach some natural and logical break in the subject-matter or until you feel drained. If you are really caught up in your work you shouldn't even notice the passage of time. And the approach to examination preparation recommended in this book is essentially an *active* one containing within itself a good deal of variety, unlike the traditional "recitation" approach. If you follow the advice contained here, you will be spending as much time planning, thinking and writing as "swotting". The constant alternation from one form of activity to another will prevent boredom – one of the prime causes of exhaustion – and keep you going.

Immediate will-power
Henry Ford once ordered his engineers to produce an eight-cylinder engine-block all in one piece. When they told him it was quite impossible, his reply was: "Well, do it anyway!" And, sure enough, they did.

Once they realised that their jobs depended on producing the engine as directed, they put their minds to it until they were able to achieve what they had previously thought an impossibility. In short, an excellent demonstration of the old adage, "Where there's a will there's a way."

But exercising will-power is often seen as a chore which is best held over till tomorrow – the tomorrow which never comes, as in the story of the barber told in Chapter II. "Tomorrow I'm going to start swotting for my examinations" makes a major production out of it and turns it into a daunting prospect. Don't think of it as a huge undertaking and, above all, don't leave it till tomorrow. Start right away, today, with some small but concrete piece of work. This will not only serve as tangible proof of your achievement but will also give you the courage and determination to carry on as you have begun. As the Chinese saying has it: "Every journey of a thousand miles begins with a single step."

Another common cause of procrastination is perfectionism. A good example is the research student who puts off writing his thesis until he has exhausted the literature in his field, which often means that he never gets around to writing it at all. It may well be that perfectionism is not so much a cause of procrastination as an excuse for not getting started – rooted in a fear of failure. After all, if you never submit your dissertation it can't be rejected!

The solution here is the same as for the all-in-one engine block: take that tiny first step now and you will be on your way. The sense of achievement which results should overcome that inner fear of failure. In short, apply *immediate will-power*.

Panic

William Gladstone, one of the most accomplished of parliamentary orators of all time, confessed that he always felt butterflies in his stomach before rising to speak in the House of Commons. In fact, a certain amount of stress does no harm and actually enhances one's performance.

One of the most nerve-racking of activities is undoubtedly playing in an orchestra: a single false note can make all the difference between success and ignominy. To alleviate the nervous tension it was recently arranged that all the members of a well-known orchestra should be given tranquillisers just before their performance. They felt very much more relaxed, but the level of their performance dropped appreciably. The players felt *so* unconcerned that they couldn't be bothered to be accurate!

Taking drugs to "calm your nerves" is certainly no more likely to improve your examination performance than your musical proficiency. You don't want to feel groggy in the examination room! What is just as bad, of course, is the taking of "pep pills" to keep you awake long enough to do all that cramming on the night before the exam. Not only will you be a zombie the next day, but if you make a habit of it you could easily become addicted, which will mean that your body will actually need higher and higher doses of the drug to reach the same state of alertness.

There is, however, a big difference between that slight nervous tension which is just enough to put an edge on one's performance and the panic terror which sometimes overcomes students just before an examination. The best antidote to panic is to follow the pattern of exam preparation recommended in this book. That way you will not only have the requisite knowledge to face the exam but, what is just as important, the *confidence* that you have it.

What exactly does it mean to "know" enough for the examination? It makes one wonder what the purpose of an examination can possibly be if so many – successful – candidates are quite unable to recall even the broad outline of the syllabus, let alone the subject matter, of an examination which they took only a few months earlier. In fact, the examination tests the state of your knowledge on one particular day and on that day only. Whether 10% of that knowledge has evaporated from the surface of your brain within twenty-four hours or whether the figure more nearly approximates 50% or even 100% is no concern of the examiners.

Because of this many students postpone their examination preparation to the last minute. Where the examination is essentially of a factual nature they may have a point, because nothing is more quickly forgotten than isolated and insignificant details. But in an examination of genuine university standard the key to success is a conceptual framework, into which the facts are then slotted, as we saw in Chapters V and VIII. To do *this* kind of preparation adequately, last-minute cramming is most certainly not enough. The bulk of the preparation should be done during the course of the year, the work in the weeks and days just before the examination being revision.

But, however thorough your earlier groundwork, don't get drunk on the night before your big examination. Reserve that

for the night after you get your results! The work done the
night before the examination can be crucial to your results,
but it should not be last-minute desperate cramming of
material you've never set eyes on before.

The day of destiny

There is really no excuse for arriving late for an examination.
If you are not quite certain where the examination venue is
or how to get there, take time off a week or two beforehand
to explore. The psychological trauma that you will suffer from
coming late could affect your performance much more than
the lateness itself.

There is also no excuse for forgetting to bring a pen and
having to go round amongst your fellow candidates begging
someone to lend you one. In fact, it is always a good idea to
have at least two pens on you, and don't start experimenting
in the examination room with that new pen which Aunt
Agatha gave you for good luck. The pen you use in the examination should be one you are used to. And, if you plan to
underline anything or rule any lines at all, a ruler is worth
taking along too, as are a pencil and rubber for any drawing
or for rough work.

In the days when I used to do some invigilating I could
never get over the number of students who would show up
at an examination without a watch. Even if there is a large
clock in the hall, it may be out of order the day you need it
or you may find yourself sitting with your back to it, so that
you will have to crane your neck round every few minutes,
thus wasting valuable time and arousing the invigilator's sus-
picions. So don't take a chance.

The timing of an examination is of course crucial, not just
as regards the overall time-limit but also the time allotted to
each question. On the whole I believe students tend to be
advised to spend too long reading through the question-paper.
Five minutes should be enough for this purpose, unless the
questions are very long indeed. The (sometimes wordy)
instructions at the head of the paper should not require more
than a passing glance, as you ought to have familiarised yourself with them long since. Your only purpose in looking over
them at all is to check that the number of questions to be
answered, the number of examination books to be used and
the like are as you expected.

This is also not the time to pore laboriously over the questions. Your five minutes are merely to enable you to select the questions you are going to answer. If this is a particularly agonising choice it may help to do it negatively, by a process of elimination. But don't, of course, make so hasty a decision that you have to change your mind half-way through attempting a question which you *thought* you could manage but which turns out to be very different from your initial impression of it. This can be a fatal mistake.

Once you have made your selection, you have to decide in which order to attempt the questions. Students are sometimes advised to answer their *second-best* question first, then their best question and then the rest, ending with the one they are least happy about. Why not start with your *best* question? you may well ask. The answer is that if you do it second you will really be in your stride by then and be able to go to town on it, having built up some confidence by doing your next strongest question already. This is fine, provided you don't spend more than *ten seconds* trying to work out which your second-best question is! If you can't decide, just start on a question you are reasonably confident about and get going.

But don't start writing your answer straightaway. First read the question carefully and analyse it as suggested in Chapter IX. It always helps to underline or highlight the key words in the question or anything that calls for special attention.

Next, jot down your mnemonic (see Chapter VIII) on some rough paper and expand it to form a proper essay plan. (If no rough paper is provided, use part of an answer sheet and cross it through.) This does *not* mean that by hook or by crook you must force the question asked into your precast mould. That could indeed be fatal. But, if you have done your homework properly you *should* have prepared a mnemonic which can be adapted to your needs in the examination room. Always make sure that the question you are answering is the one set and no other.

In a five-question three-hour paper your planning should take no more than five minutes per question, and the remaining time (less the five minutes for your initial reading of the paper) should be equally divided among the questions (assuming they all carry equal marks). This will give you 30 minutes for the actual writing of each of your answers, a limit to which you must stick religiously. If you have only four questions to answer, you can afford to spend seven or eight minutes on planning each answer and you can then allow yourself 35 minutes for each.

As any athlete will tell you, it is vital to practise in advance the distance that you are going to run on the day. It's no use practising the 100-metre dash if you are going to be running the marathon! So, don't wait until the day of the examination itself to practise your time-keeping. Try some questions under simulated examination conditions well before the time.

What about time to read over your answers? This is often recommended, but it rarely does any good. Except for the occasional trivial error, you are quite likely to miss even glaring oversights, such as an accidentally omitted "not". Which is why authors who do their own proof-reading usually don't make a particularly good job of it.

The chief purpose of reading through your work is of course to spot serious errors of substance and omissions. But if you follow the advice of this book and work from plans carefully worked out in advance, there should be no need to check for serious mistakes or major omissions. Your plan itself will serve as a checklist of all the main points in that particular answer, and it is a good idea to tick each one off as you deal with it. Also, if you follow your plan there should be no major omissions. As for the organisation of your answer, the points in your plan should be numbered according to the demands of the question set.

Post mortems

Post mortems are best avoided, especially straight after an examination. Above all, don't let an unpleasant paper depress you and put you off your stride for the rest. Rather put it out of your mind for the time being, though it may be very useful for you to go over it later, once the whole of your current batch of examinations is over. You *can* learn from your mistakes, as we saw in Chapter IV, and it is certainly useful to try. So, once your results are out there is no harm in reviewing your peformance and finding out how you can improve upon it. Remember, replace "if only" with "next time".

Also, avoid taking a fatalistic attitude. Explaining away a disastrous performance with remarks such as "I'm no good at languages" or "I *knew* I shouldn't have chosen to read Geography" will only serve to persuade you that the result was inevitable, which is very likely to become a self-fulfilling prophecy.

In 1066 both William and Harold saw what is now known as Halley's comet. William saw it as a good omen, while Harold was sure it presaged ill. Both were right. So much for "fate", a concept which tends to negate initiative, as we saw in Chapter IV.

One of the best ways of avoiding an unpleasant shock when you see your results posted up is by *studying your examiners as closely as you study your subject*. How to do this is fully discussed in Chapter I.

Theses

A thesis is really just a very long essay, and if this is constantly borne in mind it does not appear quite so formidable. Like any essay, a thesis is made up of a number of sections, which should be mapped out in advance in exactly the same way as for ordinary essays (see Chapter IX). In fact, the whole process of writing a thesis or dissertation, no matter how long or short and regardless of subject, is identical to that of writing an essay, as described in Chapter IX.

One of the commonest mistakes made by research students – and one of the main reasons for the inordinate length of time so many of them take to complete their degrees – is the idea that you must not start "writing up" until you have finished all your reading. This makes even less sense when applied to a thesis than in regard to an ordinary undergraduate essay. For one thing, the sections of a thesis are often quite separate self-contained entities, which are frequently published in isolation from one another afterwards. Secondly, it is always best to work out your thoughts while the information is fresh in your mind. Doing *all* your reading before *any* writing will make your reading much less purposeful than otherwise, will entail your taking much more copious notes than is really necessary or else will force you to do a lot of rereading in order to refamiliarise yourself with the material. It will also give you many more organisational headaches, as your notes will be so voluminous as to be quite unmanageable and inaccessible without some sort of indexing system. If, on the other hand, you were to deal with one chapter at a time, your notes for each could conveniently be confined to a single file, notebook or set of cards.

But remember, doing your writing as you go along does *not* mean that you are stuck with what you have written for all time. Regard yourself always as writing a draft: the fear of finality is enough to create a block in even the toughest of minds. And, if you have access to a word-processor, editing and rewriting is no chore anyway (see Chapter IX).

At one time certain universities insisted on a final title for your thesis as soon as you registered as a research student. This is no longer the case, so there is no excuse for choosing a topic which really does not suit you or which you find boring or pointless. Success is directly proportional to the research student's enthusiasm for his project, and the same applies to undergraduate theses, dissertations and long essays.

Don't allow your supervisor simply to hand you a topic unless you are really fired up by it as well. He may have his own ulterior motive for palming it off on you, but unless you really want to there is no reason why you should become a cog in some research wheel of his. A lot of dissertations, even at Ph.D. level, are the products of mechanical observation and compilation rather than of real original thinking. This applies not only in the natural sciences, where large research teams are usual, but also in such traditionally independent areas as the humanities. Some of the most mindless kinds of dissertations are commentaries on texts, most of which are excellent examples of not being able to see the wood for the trees. Unless you are a pedant by nature, you should avoid this kind of topic.

In general, the chief problem with the choice of a research topic is the concept of "topic" itself. If one thought in terms of questions or problems rather than "subjects" or "topics", there would be less emphasis on mindless fact-grubbing and more on thinking, which is lamentably under-represented in the majority of theses.

Guidelines

1. Don't say: "But I read my notes through 37 times!"
    Remember: reading and learning are two different things.

2. Parrot-fashion learning is fine – for parrots.

3. Remember the blind men and the elephant: details must be slotted into a framework if they are to make sense.

4. Familiarise yourself thoroughly with the syllabus. Then devise your own private syllabus.

5. Prepare short essay plans covering the whole of your syllabus.

6. Test yourself frequently – in writing. Remember: It's easier to fool yourself than anyone else in the world.

7. Become a good time-manager: prioritise your activities.

8. Remember: Adequate preparation is the best bulwark against panic.

9. Don't get drunk the night before your exam, but do some revision – not cramming.

10. Make sure you get to the exam in plenty of time.

11. Take two pens with you, and a watch.

12. Spend a maximum of five minutes reading through the paper.

13. Take no more than 10 seconds to decide which question to tackle first.

14. Now read your first question carefully and analyse it (see Chapter IX), underlining or highlighting the key words.

15. Jot down your mnemonic (see Chapter VIII).

16. Planning each answer should take no more than five minutes (in a five-question three-hour paper) or seven or eight minutes (in a four-question three-hour paper).

17. Remember: Practise answering exam questions in simulated exam conditions well in advance.

18. Avoid holding a post mortem straight after the exam. But once your results are out it can be useful to review your performance.

19. Avoid a fatalistic attitude (see Chapter IV).

20. *Theses*: Just remember that a thesis is really only an

over grown essay and you won't go wrong. But don't allow your supervisor to browbeat you into taking on a topic which doesn't suit you or which entails mindless pedantic fact-grubbing instead of genuine research, i.e. thinking.

21. **Study your examiners as closely as you study your subject.**

OUR PUBLISHING POLICY

HOW WE CHOOSE

Our policy is to consider every deserving manuscript and we can give special editorial help where an author is an authority on his subject but an inexperienced writer. We are rigorously selective in the choice of books we publish. We set the highest standards of editorial quality and accuracy. This means that a *Paperfront* is easy to understand and delightful to read. Where illustrations are necessary to convey points of detail, these are drawn up by a subject specialist artist from our panel.

HOW WE KEEP PRICES LOW

We aim for the big seller. This enables us to order enormous print runs and achieve the lowest price for you. Unfortunately, this means that you will not find in the *Paperfront* list any titles on obscure subjects of minority interest only. These could not be printed in large enough quantities to be sold for the low price at which we offer this series.

We sell almost all our *Paperfronts* at the same unit price. This saves a lot of fiddling about in our clerical departments and helps us to give you world-beating value. Under this system, the longer titles are offered at a price which we believe to be unmatched by any publisher in the world.

OUR DISTRIBUTION SYSTEM

Because of the competitive price, and the rapid turnover, *Paperfronts* are possibly the most profitable line a bookseller can handle. They are stocked by the best bookshops all over the world. It may be that your bookseller has run out of stock of a particular title. If so, he can order more from us at any time – we have a fine reputation for "same day" despatch, and we supply any order, however small (even a single copy), to any bookseller who has an account with us. We prefer you to buy from your bookseller, as this reminds him of the strong underlying public demand for *Paperfronts*. Members of the public who live in remote places, or who are housebound, or whose local bookseller is unco-operative, can order direct from us by post.

FREE

If you would like an up-to-date list of all paperfront titles currently available, send a stamped self-addressed envelope to
ELLIOT RIGHT WAY BOOKS, BRIGHTON RD.,
LOWER KINGSWOOD, SURREY, U.K.